CAPTAIN AMERICA
THE WINTER SOLDIER
PRELUDE

COLLECTION EDITOR: JENNIFER GRÜNWALD
ASSOCIATE MANAGING EDITOR: ALEX STARBUCK
EDITOR, SPECIAL PROJECTS: MARK D. BEAZLEY
MASTERWORKS EDITOR: CORY SEDLMEIER
SENIOR EDITOR, SPECIAL PROJECTS: JEFF YOUNGQUIST
SVP PRINT, SALES & MARKETING: DAVID GABRIEL

EDITOR IN CHIEF: AXEL ALONSO CHIEF CREATIVE OFFICER: JOE QUESADA
PUBLISHER: DAN BUCKLEY EXECUTIVE PRODUCER: ALAN FINE

MARVEL'S CAPTAIN AMERICA: THE WINTER SOLDIER PRELUDE. Contains material originally published in magazine form as MARVEL'S CAPTAIN AMERICA: THE FIRST AVENGER ADAPTATION #1-2, MARVEL'S CAPTAIN AMERICA: THE WINTER SOLDIER INFINITE COMIC #1, CAPTAIN AMERICA (1968) #117, CAPTAIN AMERICA (2005) #6, THE ULTIMATES #2 and TALES OF SUSPENSE (1959) #57. First printing 2014. ISBN# 978-0-7851-8877-3. Published by MARVEL WORLDWIDE, INC., a subsidiary of MARVEL ENTERTAINMENT, LLC. OFFICE OF PUBLICATION: 135 West 50th Street, New York, NY 10020. **Printed in the U.S.A.** ALAN FINE, EVP - Office of the President, Marvel Worldwide, Inc. and EVP & CMO Marvel Characters B.V.; DAN BUCKLEY, Publisher & President - Print, Animation & Digital Divisions; JOE QUESADA, Chief Creative Officer; TOM BREVOORT, SVP of Publishing; DAVID BOGART, SVP of Operations & Procurement, Publishing; C.B. CEBULSKI, SVP of Creator & Content Development; DAVID GABRIEL, SVP of Print & Digital Publishing Sales; JIM O'KEEFE, VP of Operations & Logistics; DAN CARR, Executive Director of Publishing Technology; SUSAN CRESPI, Editorial Operations Manager; ALEX MORALES, Publishing Operations Manager; STAN LEE, Chairman Emeritus. For information regarding advertising in Marvel Comics or on Marvel.com, please contact Niza Disla, Director of Marvel Partnerships, at ndisla@marvel.com. For Marvel subscription inquiries, please call 800-217-9158. **Manufactured between 1/3/2014 and 2/10/2014 by R.R. DONNELLEY, INC., SALEM, VA, USA.**

CAPTAIN AMERICA
THE FIRST AVENGER

BASED ON THE MARVEL STUDIOS FILM **CAPTAIN AMERICA: THE FIRST AVENGER**
SCREENPLAY BY **CHRISTOPHER MARKUS & STEPHEN McFEELY**

WRITER: **PETER DAVID** PENCILER: **WELLINTON ALVES**
INKERS: **MANNY CLARK, ANDERSON SILVA & WELLINTON ALVES**
COLORIST: **CHRIS SOTOMAYOR** LETTERER: **VC's CLAYTON COWLES**
ASSISTANT EDITOR: **EMILY SHAW** EDITOR: **BILL ROSEMANN**

MARVEL STUDIOS
CREATIVE MANAGER: **WILL CORONA PILGRIM**
VP PRODUCTION & DEVELOPMENT: **BRAD WINDERBAUM**
SVP PRODUCTION & DEVELOPMENT: **STEPHEN BROUSSARD**
PRESIDENT: **KEVIN FEIGE**

CAPTAIN AMERICA
THE WINTER SOLDIER

INFINITE COMIC

WRITER: **PETER DAVID** STORYBOARD ARTIST: **DANIEL GOVAR** ARTIST: **ROCK-HE KIM**
COLORIST: **RAIN BEREDO** LETTERER: **VC's CLAYTON COWLES**
ASSISTANT EDITOR: **EMILY SHAW** EDITOR: **BILL ROSEMANN**
PRODUCTION MANAGER: **TIM SMITH 3** PRODUCTION: **ARLIN ORTIZ**

MARVEL STUDIOS
CREATIVE MANAGER: **WILL CORONA PILGRIM**
SVP PRODUCTION & DEVELOPMENT: **NATE MOORE**
CREATIVE EXECUTIVE: **TRINH TRAN**
PRESIDENT: **KEVIN FEIGE**

TALES OF SUSPENSE #57

WRITER: **STAN LEE** ARTIST: **DON HECK**
LETTERER: **SAM ROSEN**
COLOR & ART RECONSTRUCTION: **TOM MULLIN**

CAPTAIN AMERICA (1968) #117

WRITER: **STAN LEE** PENCILER: **GENE COLAN**
INKER: **JOE SINNOTT** LETTERER: **SAM ROSEN**
ART RECONSTRUCTION: **DALE CRAIN**
COLOR RECONSTRUCTION: **LAURIE SMITH**

CAPTAIN AMERICA (2005) #6

WRITER: **ED BRUBAKER** ARTIST: **STEVE EPTING**
COLORIST: **FRANK D'ARMATA**
LETTERER: **VC'S RANDY GENTILE**
ASSISTANT EDITORS: **ANDY SCHMIDT, STEPHANIE MOORE & MOLLY LAZER**
EDITOR: **TOM BREVOORT**

THE ULTIMATES #2

WRITER: **MARK MILLAR** PENCILER: **BRYAN HITCH**
INKER: **ANDREW CURRIE** COLORIST: **PAUL MOUNTS**
LETTERER: **CHRIS ELIOPOULOS**
ASSOCIATE EDITOR: **BRIAN SMITH**
EDITOR: **RALPH MACCHIO**

CAPTAIN AMERICA CREATED BY **JOE SIMON** AND **JACK KIRBY**

THE WORLD EXPOSITION OF TOMORROW, MAY 1942...
WHERE A YOUNG BROOKLYN MAN NAMED STEVE ROGERS IS ABOUT TO TRY AND ENLIST...AGAIN.

YOU'RE REALLY GONNA DO THIS AGAIN?
WELL, IT'S A FAIR, BUCKY. I'M GONNA TRY MY LUCK.
THIS ISN'T A BACK ALLEY, STEVE. IT'S WAR. WHY ARE YOU SO KEEN TO FIGHT?
WHAT DO YOU WANT ME TO DO? COLLECT SCRAP METAL IN MY LITTLE RED WAGON? MEN ARE LAYING DOWN THEIR LIVES.
I CAN DO AS WELL AS THEM...

"...AND I GOT NO RIGHT TO DO ANY LESS."
I'M DOCTOR ABRAHAM ERSKINE. I REPRESENT THE STRATEGIC SCIENTIFIC RESERVE.
SO...FIVE EXAMS. IN FIVE DIFFERENT CITIES.
THAT MIGHT NOT BE THE RIGHT FILE.
NO, IT'S NOT THE EXAMS I AM INTERESTED IN. IT'S THE FIVE TRIES.

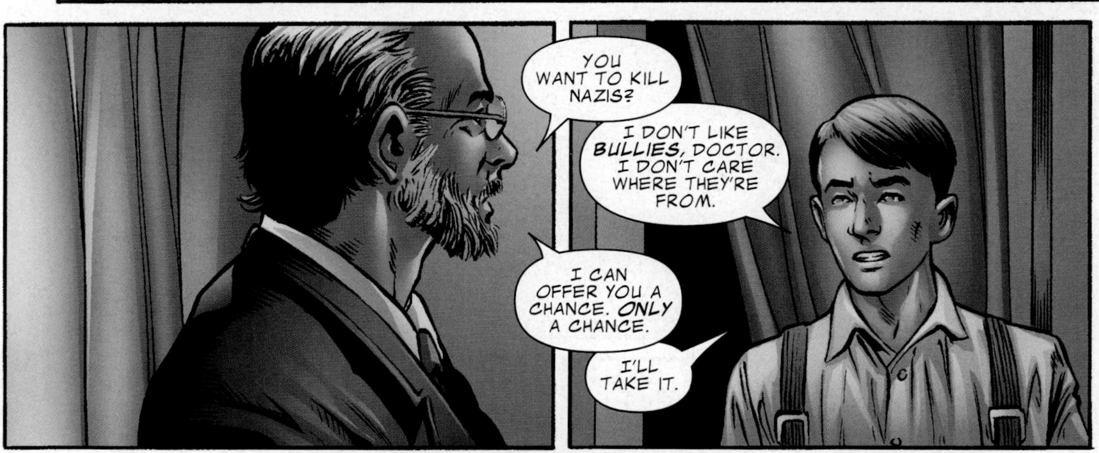

YOU WANT TO KILL NAZIS?
I DON'T LIKE BULLIES, DOCTOR. I DON'T CARE WHERE THEY'RE FROM.
I CAN OFFER YOU A CHANCE. ONLY A CHANCE.
I'LL TAKE IT.

"YOU'RE NOT REALLY THINKIN' ABOUT PICKIN' ROGERS, ARE YOU?"
"WELL, I WASN'T JUST THINKING ABOUT IT, COLONEL PHILLIPS. HE IS THE CLEAR CHOICE."
1A

WHEN YOU BROUGHT A NINETY-POUND ASTHMATIC ONTO MY ARMY BASE, I LET IT SLIDE. I THOUGHT MAYBE HE'D BE USEFUL TO YOU...LIKE A GERBIL. I NEVER THOUGHT YOU'D PICK HIM.
LOOK AT HIM. HE'S MAKIN' ME CRY.
I AM LOOKING FOR QUALITIES BEYOND THE PHYSICAL.

DO YOU KNOW HOW LONG IT TOOK TO SET UP THIS PROJECT?
I AM WELL AWARE OF YOUR EFFORTS.
THEN THROW ME A BONE. HODGE PASSED EVERY TEST WE GAVE HIM.
HE IS A BULLY.

YOU DON'T WIN WARS WITH NICENESS, DOCTOR. YOU WIN WARS WITH GUTS.

GRENADE!

EVERYBODY DOWN!

OH, IT WAS A TRAINING GRENADE.

HE'S STILL SKINNY.
UH... IS THIS A TEST?

LATER...
AFTER THE FIRST WAR, MY PEOPLE STRUGGLED...THEY FELT WEAK. SMALL. THEN HITLER COMES ALONG WITH THE MARCHING AND THE BIG SHOW...
HE HEARS OF ME, MY WORK, AND HE FINDS ME. "YOU," HE SAYS, "YOU WILL MAKE US STRONG."
I AM NOT INTERESTED. SO HE SENDS THE HEAD OF HYDRA, HIS RESEARCH DIVISION. A BRILLIANT SCIENTIST NAMED JOHANN SCHMIDT.
"SCHMIDT BECAME CONVINCED THAT A GREAT POWER HAD BEEN HIDDEN IN THE EARTH, LEFT HERE BY THE GODS, WAITING TO BE SEIZED BY A SUPERIOR MAN.
"AND WHEN HE HEARS ABOUT MY FORMULA AND WHAT IT CAN DO, HE COULD NOT RESIST. SCHMIDT HAD TO BECOME THAT SUPERIOR MAN.
"THE SERUM WAS NOT READY, BUT MORE IMPORTANT... THE MAN. THE SERUM AMPLIFIES EVERYTHING THAT IS INSIDE.
"GOOD BECOMES GREAT. BAD BECOMES WORSE."
THAT IS WHY YOU WERE CHOSEN. A STRONG MAN, HE MAY LOSE RESPECT FOR POWER IF HE HAS KNOWN IT ALL HIS LIFE.
BUT A WEAK MAN KNOWS THE VALUE OF STRENGTH... AND COMPASSION.
THANKS. I THINK.
WHATEVER HAPPENS TOMORROW, YOU MUST PROMISE ME YOU'LL STAY WHO YOU ARE. NOT A PERFECT SOLDIER, BUT A GOOD MAN.
TO THE LITTLE GUYS.

WHAT AM I DOING? YOU HAVE A PROCEDURE TOMORROW. NO FLUIDS.
WE'LL DRINK IT AFTER.

MR. STARK? HOW ARE YOUR LEVELS?
COILS ARE AT PEAK, LEVELS ARE ONE HUNDRED PERCENT. WE MAY DIM HALF THE LIGHTS IN BROOKLYN, BUT WE'RE AS READY AS WE'LL EVER BE.

WE BEGIN WITH A SERIES OF MICROINJECTIONS INTO THE SUBJECT'S MAJOR MUSCLE GROUPS.
THE SUBJECT WILL THEN BE SATURATED WITH VITA-RAYS.

SERUM INFUSION. BEGINNING IN FIVE, FOUR, THREE, TWO...ONE.
UNHHH...
NOW, MR. STARK.

TWENTY PERCENT... THIRTY... FORTY...
SIXTY... EIGHTY...

ARRRHHHH!
SHUT IT DOWN! KILL THE REACTORS, MR. STARK!
NO! DON'T! I CAN DO THIS!

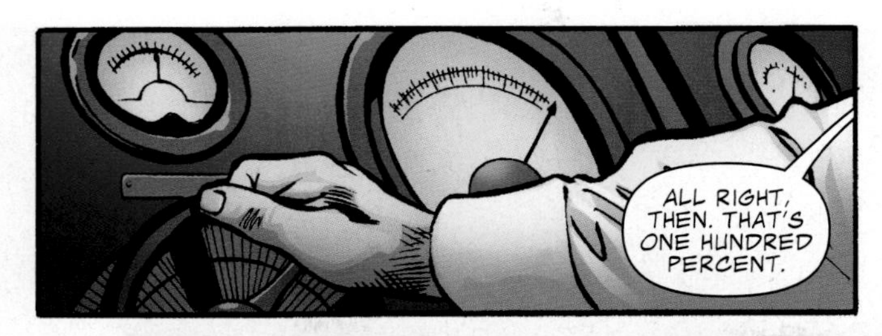
ALL RIGHT, THEN. THAT'S ONE HUNDRED PERCENT.

KZZT

MR. STARK?!

HSSSSSSSS
STEVEN?
DOCTOR? DID IT...?
I THINK... **YES.**
YOU **DID** IT, DOCTOR. YOU ACTUALLY DID IT.

BA-THOOOOOM
THAT MAN'S GOING FOR THE SERUM! STOP--!
BLAM
DOC! NO!
UNHHH...

THIS IS KRUGER, REPORTING IN. THE MISSION WAS A SUCCESS. ERSKINE IS DEAD, AND I HAVE THE--

GOTT IN HIMMEL!
KREESH

WHO THE HELL ARE YOU?!
THE FIRST OF MANY. CUT OFF ONE HEAD...

...TWO MORE SHALL TAKE ITS PLACE.
HAIL...

...Hydra...

ANY HOPE OF REPRODUCING THE PROGRAM IS LOCKED IN YOUR GENETIC CODE. BUT WITHOUT ERSKINE, IT WOULD TAKE YEARS.
AT THE MOMENT, YOU'RE THE *ONLY* SUPER-SOLDIER THERE IS.

ERSKINE DESERVED MORE THAN THAT, PEGGY.
IF IT COULD WORK ONLY ONCE, HE'D BE PROUD IT WAS YOU.

WE'RE TAKIN' THE FIGHT TO HYDRA. PACK YOUR BAGS, AGENT CARTER. YOU TOO, STARK. THE THREE OF US FLY TO LONDON TONIGHT.
SIR, IF YOU'RE GOING AFTER SCHMIDT, I WANT IN.

YOU'RE AN *EXPERIMENT*. WE'RE SENDING YOU TO ALAMAGORDO.
AS WHAT, A *LAB RAT?* THE SERUM *WORKED!*
I ASKED FOR AN ARMY AND ALL I GOT WAS YOU. YOU...ARE NOT ENOUGH.

ALL DUE RESPECT, COLONEL, HE NEEDS TO BE OUT THERE, SHOWING THE WORLD WHAT THE AMERICAN FIGHTING MAN IS MADE OF.
SON, DO YOU WANT TO SERVE YOUR COUNTRY? ON THE MOST IMPORTANT BATTLEFIELD IN THIS WAR?
THAT'S ALL I WANT, SENATOR.

THEN CONGRATULATIONS. YOU JUST GOT *PROMOTED*.

WHO'S STRONG AND BRAVE, HERE TO SAVE THE AMERICAN WAY?
NOT ALL OF US CAN STORM A BEACH OR DRIVE A TANK. BUT THERE'S STILL A WAY ALL OF US CAN FIGHT.
SERIES E DEFENSE BONDS. EACH ONE YOU BUY IS A BULLET IN THE BARREL OF YOUR BEST GUY'S GUN.
WHO VOWS TO FIGHT LIKE A MAN FOR WHAT'S RIGHT, NIGHT AND DAY?

BUFFALO
MILWAUKEE

PHILADELPHIA
CHICAGO

NOW HOW MANY OF YOU ARE READY TO HELP ME SOCK OLD ADOLF ON THE JAW?

ITALY, NOVEMBER 1943– FIVE MILES FROM THE FRONT.
OKAY...I'M GOING TO NEED A VOLUNTEER...
BRING BACK THE GIRLS!

SPLUCH
COME ON, GUYS. WE'RE ALL ON THE SAME TEAM HERE.

LATER...
THAT WAS QUITE A PERFORMANCE.
YEAH, UH, I HAD TO IMPROVISE A BIT. THE CROWDS I'M USED TO ARE USUALLY MORE... TWELVE.
I UNDERSTAND YOU ARE "AMERICA'S NEW HOPE."

PEOPLE BUY BONDS, BONDS BUY BULLETS, BULLETS KILL NAZIS. BOND SALES TAKE A TEN PERCENT BUMP IN EVERY STATE I VISIT.
IS THAT SENATOR BRANDT I HEAR?
AT LEAST BRANDT'S GOT ME DOING THIS. PHILLIPS WOULD HAVE STUCK ME IN A LAB.
AND THESE ARE YOUR ONLY OPTIONS? A LAB RAT OR DANCING MONKEY? YOU WERE MEANT FOR MORE THAN THIS.
YOU KNOW, I DREAMED ABOUT COMIN' OVERSEAS AND BEIN' ON THE FRONT LINES, SERVIN' MY COUNTRY. I FINALLY GET EVERYTHING I WANTED...
...AND I'M WEARIN' TIGHTS.

THEY LOOK LIKE THEY'VE BEEN THROUGH HELL.
THESE MEN MORE THAN MOST.
SCHMIDT SENT OUT A FORCE TO AZZANO. TWO HUNDRED MEN WENT UP AGAINST THEM. LESS THAN 50 RETURNED.

YOUR AUDIENCE CONTAINED ALL THAT'S LEFT OF THE 107th. THE REST WERE KILLED OR CAPTURED.
THE 107th?

I DON'T NEED THE WHOLE LIST. JUST ONE NAME. **SERGEANT JAMES BARNES** FROM THE 107th.
YOU DON'T GET TO GIVE ME ORDERS, "CAPTAIN."

THE NAME **DOES** SOUND FAMILIAR. I'M SORRY.
WHAT ABOUT THE OTHERS? ARE YOU PLANNING A RESCUE MISSION?
THEY ARE THIRTY MILES BEHIND THE LINES. WE'D LOSE MORE MEN THAN WE SAVE...

BUT I DON'T EXPECT YOU TO UNDERSTAND THAT, BECAUSE YOU'RE A **CHORUS GIRL.**

I THINK I UNDERSTAND JUST FINE.

THE HYDRA CAMP IS IN KRAUSBERG, TUCKED BETWEEN TWO MOUNTAIN RANGES. IT'S A FACTORY OF SOME KIND.
WE SHOULD BE ABLE TO DROP YOU RIGHT ON THE DOORSTEP.

YOU KNOW, YOU TWO ARE GONNA BE IN A LOT OF TROUBLE WHEN YOU LAND.
AND YOU WON'T?
WHERE I'M GOIN', IF ANYBODY YELLS AT ME, I CAN JUST SHOOT 'EM.
ACTIVATE YOUR TRANSPONDER WHEN YOU'RE READY AND THE SIGNAL WILL LEAD US STRAIGHT TO YOU.

I THINK WE'VE BEEN NOTICED! WE'RE BEING FIRED ON.

STEVE! GET BACK HERE! WE'RE TAKING YOU ALL THE WAY IN!
YOU CAN'T GIVE ME ORDERS!
AS SOON AS I'M CLEAR, YOU TURN THIS THING AROUND AND GET OUT OF HERE!

THE HELL I CAN'T!
I'M A CAPTAIN!

HURRY! HURRY!

WE HAVE ORDERS TO UNLOAD THIS TRUCK...

UUUNNNFFFFFF!

OOOFFF!

WHO ARE YOU SUPPOSED TO BE?
I'M...CAPTAIN AMERICA.
I BEG YOUR PARDON?

IS THERE ANYBODY ELSE?
THERE'S AN ISOLATION WARD IN THE FACTORY, BUT NO ONE'S EVER COME BACK FROM IT.
ALL RIGHT. THE TREE LINE IS NORTHWEST, EIGHTY YARDS PAST THE GATE. GET OUT FAST AND GIVE 'EM HELL. I'LL MEET YOU GUYS IN THE CLEARING WITH ANYBODY ELSE I FIND.

WAIT. YOU KNOW WHAT YOU'RE DOIN'?
YEAH. I'VE KNOCKED OUT ADOLF HITLER OVER TWO HUNDRED TIMES.

ARRHH!
UNNF!
WHAM

DOCTOR, PREPARE TO EVACUATE.
I'M SURE OUR FORCES CAN HANDLE--
OUR FORCES ARE OUTMATCHED.
PREPARE TO DESTROY THE FACTORY.

Barnes, James Buchanan. Sergeant. 3-2-5-5-7-0-3-8.
BUCKY?

WHO... WHO IS THAT? IS THAT...?
IT'S ME, BUCK.
STEVE?
I THOUGHT YOU WERE DEAD.
I THOUGHT YOU WERE SMALLER. WHAT HAPPENED TO YOU?
I JOINED THE ARMY.

DID IT HURT?
LITTLE BIT.
IS IT PERMANENT?
SO FAR.

DAMN! THIS WHOLE PLACE IS GOING UP!
COME ON! THERE'S A CATWALK OVER ON THE OTHER SIDE!

CAPTAIN AMERICA! HOW EXCITING! I AM A GREAT FAN OF YOUR FILMS. SO...
...DOCTOR ERSKINE MANAGED IT AFTER ALL. NOT EXACTLY AN IMPROVEMENT, BUT STILL... IMPRESSIVE.
YOU GOT NO IDEA!
WHUD
HAVEN'T I?
KLANG
KRAK

ERSKINE SAID YOUR EXPERIMENT WAS A FAILURE!

NO MATTER WHAT LIES ERSKINE TOLD YOU... I WAS HIS GREATEST SUCCESS!

YOU ARE DELUDED, CAPTAIN. YOU PRETEND TO BE A SIMPLE SOLDIER. BUT IN REALITY YOU ARE JUST AFRAID TO ADMIT THAT WE HAVE LEFT HUMANITY BEHIND!
UNLIKE YOU, I EMBRACE IT PROUDLY! WITHOUT FEAR!

THEN HOW COME YOU'RE RUNNING?
YOU DON'T HAVE ONE OF THOSE, DO YOU?
COME ON! THERE'S A GANTRY UP THERE! RUN!

THERE'S GOT TO BE A ROPE OR SOMETHIN'!
JUST GO! GET OUT OF HERE!
NO! NOT WITHOUT YOU!

AW, HELL.

I CAN'T TOUCH STARK. HE'S RICH...

...AND HE'S THE ARMY'S NUMBER ONE WEAPONS CONTRACTOR. YOU ARE NEITHER ONE.
WITH RESPECT, SIR, I DON'T REGRET MY ACTIONS. AND I DON'T THINK CAPTAIN ROGERS DID, EITHER.
WHAT MAKES YOU THINK I GIVE A DAMN ABOUT YOUR OPINIONS?

I TOOK A CHANCE WITH YOU, AGENT CARTER. NOW AMERICA'S GOLDEN BOY-- AND A LOT OF OTHER GOOD MEN-- ARE DEAD, 'CAUSE YOU HAD A CRUSH.
IT WASN'T THAT. I HAD FAITH.

WELL, I HOPE THAT'S A BIG COMFORT TO YOU WHEN THEY SHUT THIS DIVISION D--WHAT THE HELL IS GOIN' ON OUT THERE?

LOOK WHO IT IS!
I'LL BE DAMNED.

COLONEL, SOME OF THESE MEN NEED MEDICAL ATTENTION.

I'D LIKE TO SURRENDER MYSELF FOR DISCIPLINARY ACTION.

THAT WON'T BE NECESSARY.

YES, SIR.

FAITH, HUH?

YOU'RE LATE.
TRANSPONDER BROKE. COULDN'T CALL MY RIDE.

HEY! LET'S HEAR IT FOR CAPTAIN AMERICA!
HEY, CAP! LOOK OVER HERE!
YOU'RE THE BEST, CAP!

MARVEL'S CAPTAIN AMERICA: THE FIRST AVENGER ADAPTATION #2

S.S.R. H.Q. WAR ROOM.
THE FOURTH ONE WAS HERE IN POLAND, RIGHT NEAR THE BALTIC. AND THE LAST WAS OUTSIDE OF STRASBOURG, SAY THIRTY, FORTY MILES WEST OF THE MAGINOT LINE.
I JUST GOT A QUICK LOOK.
WELL, NOBODY'S PERFECT.

AGENT CARTER, COORDINATE WITH MI6. I WANT EVERY ALLIED EYEBALL LOOKIN' FOR THAT MAIN HYDRA BASE.
WHAT ABOUT US?
WE ARE GONNA SET A FIRE UNDER JOHANN SCHMIDT'S ASS.

WHAT DO YOU SAY, ROGERS? IT'S YOUR MAP. YOU THINK YOU CAN WIPE HYDRA OFF OF IT?
"SO LET ME GET THIS STRAIGHT..."

THE WHIP & FIDDLE PUB.
...WE BARELY GOT OUT OF THERE ALIVE AND YOU WANT US TO GO BACK?
PRETTY MUCH, DUGAN.
SOUNDS RATHER FUN, ACTUALLY. WHAT DO YOU THINK, MORITA?
BUUUUURP! I'M IN.

I'LL FIGHT. HELL, I'LL ALWAYS FIGHT. BUT YOU GOT TO DO ONE THING FOR ME.
WHAT'S THAT?
OPEN A TAB.

HOW ABOUT YOU, BUCKY? ARE YOU READY TO FOLLOW CAPTAIN AMERICA INTO THE JAWS OF DEATH?
HELL NO.
THAT LITTLE GUY FROM BROOKLYN WHO WAS TOO DUMB NOT TO RUN AWAY FROM A FIGHT? I'M FOLLOWING HIM.

CARBON POLYMER. SHOULD WITHSTAND YOUR AVERAGE GERMAN BAYONET. OF COURSE, UH, HYDRA'S NOT GONNA ATTACK YOU WITH A POCKET KNIFE.
NOW AS FOR YOUR SHIELD...
S.S.R. H.Q.
HOWARD STARK'S LAB.

...I HEAR YOU'RE, UH, KIND OF ATTACHED. I TOOK THE LIBERTY OF COMING UP WITH SOME OPTIONS.

WHAT ABOUT THIS ONE?
NO--NO, THAT'S JUST A PROTOTYPE. VIBRANIUM; IT'S STRONGER THAN STEEL AND A THIRD THE WEIGHT. IT'S THE RAREST METAL ON EARTH. WHAT YOU'RE HOLDING THERE, THAT'S ALL WE'VE GOT.

WHAT DO YOU THINK?

BLAM BLAM BLAM

YES, I THINK IT WORKS.

FRANCE, DECEMBER 1943.
BELGIUM, JANUARY 1944.
CZECHOSLOVAKIA, FEBRUARY 1944.
THE LOCATIONS CHANGE, BUT THE RESULTS REMAIN THE SAME...

...MUCH TO THE DISTRESS OF SOME, LIKE JOHANN SCHMIDT.
YOU ARE FAILING, DR. ZOLA! WE ARE CLOSE TO AN OFFENSIVE THAT WILL SHAKE THE PLANET. AND YET WE ARE CONTINUALLY DELAYED BECAUSE YOU CANNOT OUTWIT A SIMPLETON WITH A SHIELD!
FINISH YOUR MISSION, DOCTOR... BEFORE THE AMERICAN FINISHES HIS.

WE WERE RIGHT. DOCTOR ZOLA'S ON THE TRAIN. HYDRA DISPATCHER GAVE HIM PERMISSION TO OPEN UP THE THROTTLE. WHEREVER HE'S GOIN', THEY MUST NEED HIM BAD.
THE DANUBE RIVER.

THIS IS A VERY SHORT, VERY FAST TRAIN. WE'VE GOT ABOUT A TEN SECOND WINDOW! YOU MISS THAT WINDOW, WE'RE BUGS ON A WINDSHIELD!
BETTER GET MOVIN', BUGS!

REMEMBER WHEN I MADE YOU RIDE THE CYCLONE AT CONEY ISLAND?
YEAH, AND I THREW UP?

THIS ISN'T PAYBACK, IS IT?
NOW, BUCKY, WHY WOULD I DO THAT?

ALL RIGHT, GENTLEMEN! MIND THE GAP!

JONES SHOULD BE WITH US.
THAT'S A HELL OF A--
HE'S GOING TO TRY TO GET TO THE FRONT ON THE ROOF.

UH-OH. COMPANY.

UNNFFF!
CHOOM CHOOM

FIRE AGAIN! KILL HIM NOW!

STEVE, GET BEHIND ME!

BUCKY!

UNFFF!
CHOOM

NO!

THAT'S THE LAST LIFE YOU'LL TAKE.

STOP HIM! *FIRE AGAIN!*
NO! *NO!*

YES.
AND STOP THIS TRAIN.

S.S.R. H.Q. INTERROGATION CELL.
"GIVEN THE VALUABLE INFORMATION HE HAS PROVIDED, AND IN EXCHANGE FOR HIS FULL COOPERATION, DOCTOR ZOLA IS BEING REMANDED TO SWITZERLAND..."
I SENT THAT MESSAGE TO WASHINGTON THIS MORNING. OF COURSE, IT WAS ENCODED. YOU GUYS HAVEN'T BROKEN THOSE CODES, HAVE YOU? THAT WOULD BE AWKWARD...

SCHMIDT WILL KNOW THIS IS A LIE.
HE'S GONNA KILL YOU ANYWAY, ZOLA. YOU'RE A *LIABILITY.* YOU KNOW MORE ABOUT SCHMIDT THAN ANYONE.
IT'S YOU OR SCHMIDT. THAT'S JUST THE HAND YOU'VE BEEN DEALT.

SCHMIDT BELIEVES HE WALKS IN THE FOOTSTEPS OF THE *GODS.* ONLY THE WORLD *ITSELF* WILL SATISFY HIM.

YOU *DO* REALIZE THAT'S NUTS, DON'T YOU?
THE SANITY OF THE PLAN IS OF NO CONSEQUENCE.
AND WHY IS THAT?

BECAUSE HE CAN DO IT!
WHAT'S HIS TARGET?

HIS TARGET...IS *EVERYWHERE.*

WHAT REMAINS OF THE WHIP & FIDDLE PUB.
IT WASN'T YOUR FAULT.
DID YOU READ THE REPORT?
YES.
THEN YOU KNOW THAT'S NOT TRUE.

I GOT IN OVER MY HEAD. BUCKY WADED IN AND PULLED ME OUT, JUST LIKE HE ALWAYS DID. AND THE ONE TIME HE NEEDED ME TO RETURN THE FAVOR, I COULDN'T.

DID YOU BELIEVE IN YOUR FRIEND? DID YOU RESPECT HIM?
OF COURSE.
THEN STOP BLAMING YOURSELF. ALLOW BARNES THE DIGNITY OF HIS CHOICE. HE DAMN WELL MUST HAVE THOUGHT YOU WERE WORTH IT.

AS SOON AS I FINISH THIS, I'M GOING AFTER JOHANN SCHMIDT. I'M GOING TO BURN OUT EVERY HOLE THERE IS FOR HIM TO HIDE IN.
AND I'M NOT GONNA STOP UNTIL ALL OF HYDRA IS DEAD OR CAPTURED.

YOU WON'T BE ALONE.

JOHANN SCHMIDT BELONGS IN A *NUTHOUSE*. HE THINKS HE'S A GOD AND HE'S WILLING TO BLOW UP HALF THE WORLD TO PROVE IT.

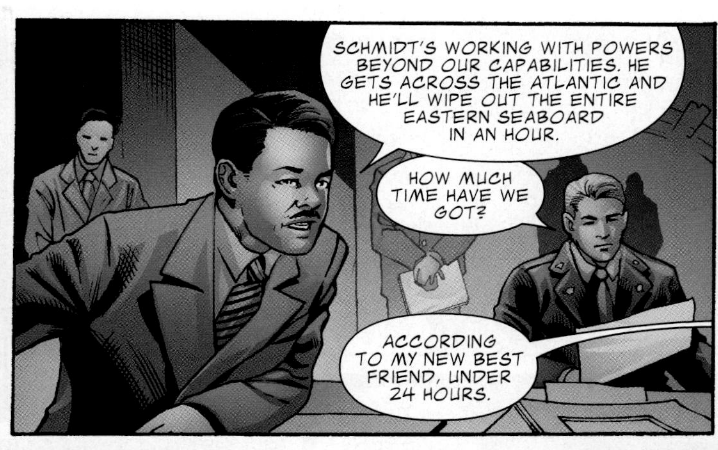
SCHMIDT'S WORKING WITH POWERS BEYOND OUR CAPABILITIES. HE GETS ACROSS THE ATLANTIC AND HE'LL WIPE OUT THE ENTIRE EASTERN SEABOARD IN AN HOUR.
HOW MUCH TIME HAVE WE GOT?
ACCORDING TO MY NEW BEST FRIEND, UNDER 24 HOURS.

HYDRA'S LAST BASE IS HERE, IN THE ALPS...
FIVE HUNDRED FEET BELOW THE SURFACE.

WHAT ARE WE SUPPOSED TO *DO?* IT'S NOT LIKE WE CAN JUST KNOCK ON THE FRONT DOOR.
WHY NOT?

"THAT'S *EXACTLY* WHAT WE'RE GOING TO DO."

"SO..."

...ARROGANCE MAY NOT BE A UNIQUELY AMERICAN TRAIT...
...BUT I MUST SAY, YOU DO IT BETTER THAN ANYONE.
THERE ARE LIMITS TO WHAT EVEN YOU CAN DO, CAPTAIN. OR DID ERSKINE TELL YOU OTHERWISE?
HE TOLD ME YOU WERE INSANE.

AH. HE RESENTED MY GENIUS. YET HE GAVE YOU EVERYTHING. WHAT MADE YOU SO SPECIAL?

NOTHIN'. I'M JUST A KID FROM BROOKLYN. I CAN DO THIS ALL DAY.

OH, OF COURSE YOU CAN. BUT UNFORTUNATELY I AM ON A TIGHT SCHEDULE.
SO AM I.

WE'RE IN! ASSAULT TEAM, GO!
KREESH

MOVE OUT!

BLAM
BLAM

YOU MIGHT NEED THIS, ROGERS.

THANKS!

BLAM BLAM

SCHMIDT'S GETTING AWAY!

GET IN!

CLOSER!
WORKING ON IT!

I'M NOT KISSING YOU.

WHEN YOU'RE DONE, I'M TAKING YOU **DANCING**. NOW...GO GET HIM.

GOT IT!

YOU DON'T GIVE UP, DO YOU?
NOPE.

AND HE'S CIRCLING THE BASES, CROSSING THIRD...

HE'S HEADING FOR HOME! AND HE MADE IT! HE MADE IT!

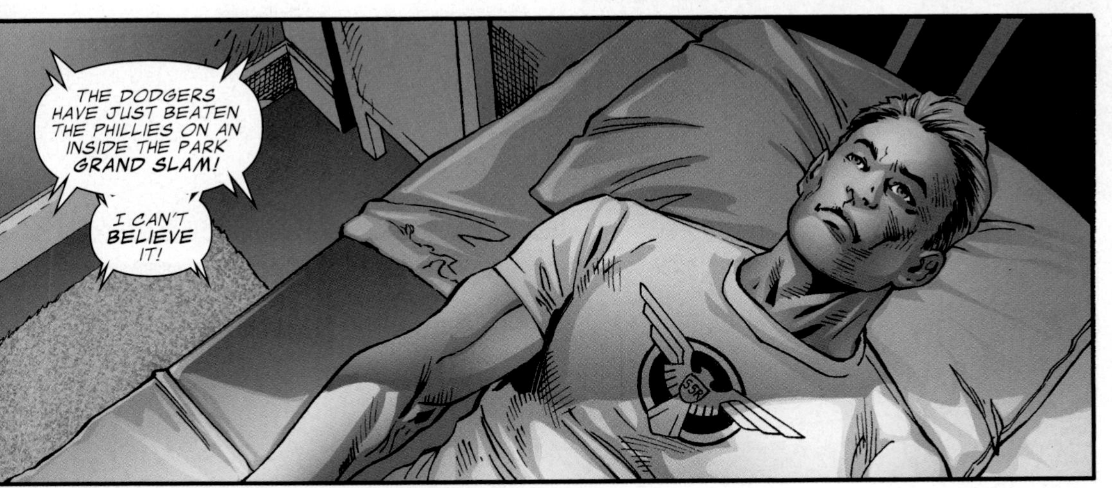
THE DODGERS HAVE JUST BEATEN THE PHILLIES ON AN INSIDE THE PARK GRAND SLAM!
I CAN'T BELIEVE IT!

GOOD MORNING, CAPTAIN ROGERS. OR SHOULD I SAY, AFTERNOON.

WHERE AM I?
YOU'RE IN A RECOVERY ROOM IN NEW YORK CITY.
WHERE AM I REALLY?
I'M AFRAID I DON'T UNDERSTAND...

THE GAME. IT'S FROM MAY 1941. I KNOW 'CAUSE I WAS THERE.
NOW I'M GOING TO ASK YOU AGAIN: WHERE AM I?

UNNNHH!

CAPTAIN ROGERS, WAIT!

ALL AGENTS, CODE 13!

WHAT IN THE--?
AT EASE, SOLDIER!

I'M SORRY ABOUT THAT LITTLE SHOW BACK THERE, BUT WE THOUGHT IT BEST TO BREAK IT TO YOU SLOWLY.
BREAK WHAT?
YOU'VE BEEN ASLEEP, CAP. FOR ALMOST SEVENTY YEARS.
NICK FURY,
DIRECTOR OF S.H.I.E.L.D.
YOU GONNA BE OKAY?
YEAH, I JUST...

...I HAD A DATE.

MARVEL'S CAPTAIN AMERICA: THE WINTER SOLDIER INFINITE COMIC #1

CHICAGO.
THE WILLIS TOWER,
SHORTLY BEFORE DAWN.
NOTE: THIS STORY TAKES PLACE BETWEEN THE EVENTS OF THE FILMS MARVEL'S THE AVENGERS AND MARVEL'S CAPTAIN AMERICA: THE WINTER SOLDIER.
WELL WELL. YOU GUYS ARE GETTING AN EARLY START TODAY...
WAIT. ARE YOU A NEW CLEANING CREW?
S'RIGHT. DON'T WORRY ABOUT US.
WELL, THE JOB SAYS I KIND OF HAVE TO.

I.D.S, PLEASE?
SURE.

GOT IT RIGHT HERE.
WHA--? NO!

PHWT PHWT
OKAY, WILSON. GET IN POSITION.
REST OF YOU, WITH ME.
I STILL DON'T UNDERSTAND WHY WE NEED A DOZEN GUYS FOR THIS OPERATION.
IF YOU DON'T THINK S.H.I.E.L.D. ISN'T GOING TO TRY AND GET BACK WHAT WE STOLE, YOU'RE KIDDING YOURSELF.
THAT'S RIDICULOUS. THEY COULDN'T POSSIBLY KNOW WHERE IT IS.

FINE. I'M RIDICULOUS.
NEXT STOP...
"...SKYDECK."
FAN OUT. MAKE SURE THERE'S NO ONE ELSE HERE.
STILL PARANOID ABOUT S.H.I.E.L.D.?
IT'S LIKE THE OLD JOKE: JUST 'CAUSE YOU'RE PARANOID...
DOESN'T MEAN THEY'RE *NOT* OUT TO GET YOU, YEAH, I KNOW.

HARD TO BELIEVE THIS LITTLE TUBE CAN CAUSE SO MUCH DAMAGE.
NOW WHAT?
NOW WE WAIT. WE WAIT FOR THE DAY TO START.
WE WAIT FOR THE SKYSCRAPER TO BE FILLED WITH THOUSANDS OF PEOPLE.
AND THEN WE RELEASE THE ZODIAC.
HEY THERE. I'M *COUGH! COUGH!* LOOKING FOR WRIGLEY FIELD.
WELL, IT'S OBVIOUSLY NOT IN HERE.
OH, SURE, I KNOW THAT.

I THINK YOU'D BETTER HEAD BACK OUT.
YOU'D TALK THAT WAY TO A ❊COUGH! COUGH❊ CUBS FAN?
YEAH, OKAY, THAT'S IT. YOU'RE HEADING OUT RIGHT N--
KLAAAANG
NICE BIT OF ACTING WORK, RUMLOW. I USED TO DO SOME OF THAT FOR THE USO.
WHERE DO YOU THINK I LEARNED IT, CAPTAIN? THEY SHOWED US YOUR OLD NEWSREELS DURING TRAINING.
WELL, NOW IT'S TIME TO SHOW ME WHAT ELSE THEY TAUGHT YOU.
YOU'D BE SURPRISED.

WE SHOULDN'T EVEN BE HERE. THESE PEOPLE--WHOEVER THEY ARE--STOLE THE ZODIAC FROM S.H.I.E.L.D....

...AFTER S.H.I.E.L.D. SWORE THEY DIDN'T HAVE IT.

AND NOW THEY *DON'T*. AND *WE'RE* GETTING IT BACK.
TOP FLOOR, RIGHT?

INCOMING ELEVATOR! OPEN FIRE!
DING

BUDDA
BUDDA
BUDDA
BUDDA

THE HELL--?
EMPTY?
NOT QUITE.
UNFFF!
WHUD
THERE'S A HUGE REWARD FOR CAPTAIN AMERICA... WE TAKE HIM ALIVE...
BUT KILL THE FRIEND!

WELL, THAT'S JUST RUDE.
THE KNIFE MAN...
I GOT HIM. YOU HANDLE THE REST.
KTANG
DONE.
KLANG
UGH!
CHUNK
BAKER! WE HAVE COMPANY.

WHAM

NO!

GIVE ME THE CASE!
ARE YOU INSANE?! LET GO OF MY RIPCORD...WE'LL BOTH DIE!

THEN WE DIE HAVING STOPPED YOU!

FINE! HERE! TAKE IT, YOU LUNATIC!

FWIZZZZ

GOT HIM!
PULL HIM UP, RUMLOW! SLOWLY... SLOWLY!
GOOD SHOT, RUMLOW.
TOLD YOU I LEARNED FROM YOU.
S.H.I.E.L.D. SAID THIS WAS DESTROYED. NO ONE'S TOLD ME WHY THEY LIED ABOUT IT.
S.H.I.E.L.D. LABELED IT AS DESTROYED SO THAT NO ONE WOULD COME LOOKING FOR IT.
A LIE, YES...BUT WELL INTENTIONED.
AND SOMEONE SAW THROUGH IT.
SO YOU'LL JUST HAVE TO STAY ON YOUR TOES, SOLDIER.

MARVEL

4.4.14

facebook.com/captainamericamovie

TALES OF SUSPENSE
featuring
THE POWER OF
IRON MAN
APPROVED BY THE COMICS CODE AUTHORITY
IND.
MARVEL COMICS GROUP 12¢
57 SEPT

HOW CAN ONE MAN WITH A STRANGE BOW AND ARROW HARM OL' SHELL-HEAD? DON'T TRY TO ANSWER TILL YOU'VE SEEN THE SENSATIONAL HAWKEYE
WE THINK HAWKEYE IS SO TERRIFIC, WE PLASTERED HIM ALL OVER OUR COVER!!
WATCH THE SPARKS FLY WHEN HANDSOME Hawkeye TEAMS UP WITH THE BLACK WIDOW!

IRON MAN
FACES THE FANTASTIC THREAT OF:
"HAWKEYE, the MARKSMAN!"
LOOK OUT, FELLA! YOU'RE NOT ALLOWED TO TAKE HOT SHOWERS ON COMPANY TIME!
WE HAVEN'T BEGUN A STORY WITH IRON MAN SAVING SOMEONE'S LIFE LATELY! SO LET'S DO IT NOW! IN THE HUGE WEAPONS FACTORY OF WEALTHY TONY STARK, A VAT OF MOLTEN STEEL ACCIDENTALLY TIPS TOWARDS A WORKMAN BELOW, WHEN IRON MAN, STARK'S PERSONAL BODYGUARD, LEAPS TO THE RESCUE! (AND ONLY WE KNOW THAT IRON MAN AND STARK ARE ONE AND THE SAME!)
WRITTEN BY: Smiling STAN LEE
ILLUSTRATED BY: Sparkling DON HECK
LETTERED BY: Sterling S.ROSEN
X-742

YOU'LL BE ALL RIGHT NOW, PARKER! NEXT TIME BE CAREFUL WHERE YOU STOP TO TIE YOUR SHOE-LACE!
I SURE WILL, IRON MAN! BOY! AM I GLAD MR. STARK HAS YOU ON THE PAYROLL!
HEY, IRON MAN! GOT A MINUTE?

WHAT CAN I DO FOR YOU, HAPPY? SOMETHING WRONG IN THE FRONT OFFICE?
NAH, THIS IS PERSONAL! YOU'RE PRETTY CHUMMY WITH MR. STARK! HOW ABOUT ASKIN' HIM TO PUT IN A GOOD WORD WITH PEPPER FOR ME! SHE HASN'T GIVEN ME A DATE IN WEEKS!

LATER, IN STARK'S PRIVATE OFFICE...
WHY SHOULD I FEEL SO JEALOUS WHEN HAPPY TRIES TO DATE PEPPER?? AFTER ALL... I DON'T DARE GET SERIOUS ABOUT HER!
A MAN LIKE ME... WHOSE LIFE DEPENDS ON A TRANSISTOR-POWERED CHEST DEVICE KEEPING HIS INJURED HEART BEATING, CAN'T VERY WELL ALLOW ROMANCE TO ENTER HIS LIFE!

AND SO, TONY STARK BEGINS TO SPEAK TO HIS LOVELY SECRETARY...
PEPPER, I HAVE SOMETHING TO ASK YOU! IT'S ABOUT A DATE...
A DATE??

OH, MR. STARK! I WAS BEGINNING TO THINK YOU'D NEVER NOTICE ME! I'M SO THRILLED!
WAIT! LET ME EXPLAIN!

WHAT'S THERE TO EXPLAIN? YOU ASKED ME FOR A DATE... AND I SAY YES!! NOW LET'S SEE... WHAT WILL I WEAR...?
BUT-- I WAS SPEAKING FOR HAPPY!

'SCUSE ME, BOSS! I... DIDN'T MEAN TO... INTERRUPT!
HAPPY...!
2.

LATER THAT NIGHT, ON THE MIDWAY AT CONEY ISLAND...
THIS ISN'T THE STORK CLUB... BUT AT LEAST I'M ON A DATE WITH TONY STARK!
I DON'T DARE TRUST MYSELF TO TAKE HER TO ANY PLACE MORE ROMANTIC THAN THIS!
HURRY! HURRY! HURRY!
STEP RIGHT UP, FOLKS! SEE HAWK-EYE, THE WONDER OF THE AGE! THE WORLD'S GREATEST MARKSMAN!
THIS IS PERFECT! AT LEAST IT'LL KEEP HER FROM SUGGESTING A RIDE IN THE TUNNEL OF LOVE!
BIG DEAL! SO HE HIT THE TARGET!! WHAT A CRUMMY ACT!
C'MON! GET THAT BUM OFF THE STAGE AND BRING ON THE DANCIN' GIRLS!

BUT THE EVENING IS DESTINED TO BE MORE NERVE-WRACKING THAN ANYONE SUSPECTS! FOR, AT THAT VERY MOMENT...
HELP!! GET US DOWN FROM HERE!!
THE FLYING PINWHEEL IS OUT OF CONTROL! WE CAN'T STOP IT!

WHY DOESN'T SOMEBODY DO SOMETHING! IF THAT THING EVER BREAKS APART...!
THIS IS TERRIBLE! NOBODY CAN STOP IT IN TIME!
PEPPER... EXCUSE ME FOR A MINUTE!! I'VE GOT TO CALL THE FACTORY!!
AT A TIME LIKE THIS!?

BUT, AS TONY STARK HASTILY SLIPS AWAY...
SNA-A-AP!
HELP!! THE GEARS ARE SHATTERING!!

AND THEN...
I'M GLAD I BROUGHT MY SPECIAL ATTACHÉ CASE WITH ME FROM THE OFFICE! I WAS ABLE TO CHANGE TO IRON MAN IN SECONDS!
AND NOW, I'VE GOT TO FIND A WAY TO STOP THAT MACHINE, ALONE AND UNAIDED!

FOR LONG GRUELLING SECONDS, THE MAN OF IRON HOLDS ON GRIMLY... KNOWING THAT HUMAN LIVES HANG IN THE BALANCE! AND THEN, SLOWLY, EXCRUCIATINGLY, THE GIANT MACHINE GRINDS TO A HALT...

I KNOW... I'LL TELL PEPPER I WENT TO FIND IRON MAN... I'LL SAY HE HAD ORDERS TO FOLLOW US TO CONEY ISLAND!

SHE'S SURE TO BELIEVE IT! MOST EVERYBODY THINKS IRON MAN ALWAYS TAGS ALONG BEHIND ME **ANYWAY!**

MEANTIME, THERE IS **ONE** OBSERVER WHO FEELS NO JOY AT WHAT HAS HAPPENED! THE ONLY EMOTION HE EXPERIENCES IS ONE OF BURNING, BLAZING **JEALOUSY!**

WHY COULDN'T ***I*** DO ALL THE THINGS IRON MAN CAN DO?? ALL IT TAKES ARE A LOT OF MECHANICAL GIMMICKS... AND A COLORFUL COSTUME DISGUISE!

AND SO, WE ARE ABOUT TO WITNESS THE CREATION OF ONE OF THE MOST START-LING ARCH-VILLAINS OF ALL TIME!!

A SHORT TIME LATER, IN A BASEMENT WORKSHOP, THE BROODING MARKSMAN WORKS FEVERISHLY...

NIGHT TURNS TO DAY, AND BACK TO NIGHT AGAIN, AND STILL THE FANATICAL MAN WORKS WITH A DESPERATE ZEAL...
BUT A COSTUME IS ONLY PART OF IT! I'LL NEED WEAPONS!

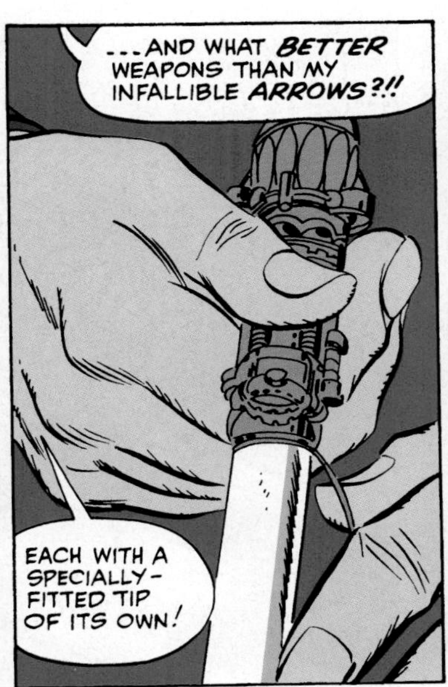
...AND WHAT BETTER WEAPONS THAN MY INFALLIBLE ARROWS?!!
EACH WITH A SPECIALLY-FITTED TIP OF ITS OWN!

NEVER AGAIN WILL PEOPLE SNEER AT MY "PERFORMANCE"!

AND NOW, INASMUCH AS MOST OTHER COSTUMED ADVENTURERS CHOOSE TO WEAR MASKS, HAWKEYE WILL DO THE SAME!

SO, LET IRON MAN... AND EVERY COSTUMED ADVENTURER LOOK TO HIS LAURELS!! FOR HAWKEYE IS ABOUT TO MAKE THEM ALL LOOK SICK!

ALTHOUGH I POSSESS NO SUPER-POWERS OTHER THAN MY UNFAILING ACCURACY AT TARGET SHOOTING, I CAN DO WHATEVER OTHERS CAN DO BY MEANS OF MY ARROWS!
FOR INSTANCE, IF I SHOULD WANT TO "FLY" TO THAT ROOF-TOP...

MY SUCTION TIPPED ARROW STICKS TO THE EXACT SPOT I AIM FOR, AND THEN...
...MY SPRING PULLEY DEVICE WHISKS ME TOWARDS THE ARROW TIP IN JUST SECONDS...

WHAT A THRILL!! I FEEL AS THOUGH THE DESTINY OF THE ENTIRE CITY BELOW ME IS IN MY POWERFUL GLOVED HANDS!

THIS IS ALMOST TOO GOOD TO BE TRUE! RIGHT BELOW ME... THAT FLEEING FOOL JUST ROBBED A JEWELRY STORE!
I CAN STOP HIM WITH MY EYES CLOSED!!

FOR THE LUVVA PETE!!
THANG!
A PERFECT SHOT!! AS ALWAYS!!

NOW TO MAKE THE CAPTURE AND... WHA..? HE'S GETTING AWAY!
THAT'S WHAT I GET FOR TAKING PAINS NOT TO INJURE HIM!!

WELL, I'LL CATCH UP WITH HIM IN A MINUTE! FIRST, I'LL JUST INSPECT WHAT HE DROPPED!
NO WONDER HE RAN SO FAST! THIS IS QUITE A HAUL! DIAMONDS... RUBIES...

JUST THEN, AN IRONIC DEVELOPMENT OCCURS! ATTRACTED BY THE NOISE, THE POLICE ARRIVE, AND...
DON'T MOVE!! WE CAUGHT YOUR PARTNER, AND WE'VE GOT YOU DEAD TO RIGHTS!
THEY THINK I HELPED ROB THE STORE!
6.

DROPPING THE STOLEN JEWELRY, HAWKEYE BEGINS A MAD DASH FOR FREEDOM AS THE OFFICERS TAKE UP THE CHASE...
THEY'D NEVER BELIEVE I'M INNOCENT! I'LL HAVE TO RUN FOR IT!
HALT... IN THE NAME OF THE LAW!
LOOK! HE DROPPED THE LOOT! WE'D BETTER PICK IT UP BEFORE SOMEONE HELPS HIMSELF TO IT!

AND, AS HAWKEYE TAKES ADVANTAGE OF THE MOMENTARY RESPITE...
THAT MAN... RACING SO SWIFTLY! HE MIGHT BE WHAT I'M LOOKING FOR!

WHY RUN WHEN YOU CAN RIDE!? SHUT THE DOOR BEHIND YOU!
JUST WHAT I NEED... A LIFT! BUT, WHY DID SHE STOP FOR ME..??

LOOK, LADY... I.. WOW!!
WHAT IS WRONG? IS SOMETHING THE MATTER?!
AS FATE WOULD HAVE IT, HAWKEYE SEES ONE OF THE MOST BEAUTIFUL WOMEN IN THE WORLD...

...THE DARING, DAZZLING DANGEROUS BLACK WIDOW!!
LADY, WHOEVER YOU ARE, DON'T PINCH ME! THIS IS ONE DREAM I DON'T EVER WANT TO WAKE UP FROM!
I ASSURE YOU, MY COSTUMED FRIEND, THIS IS NO DREAM!

IF YOU ARE AS ADVENTUROUS AND POWERFUL AS YOUR APPEARANCE WOULD INDICATE, YOU MIGHT BE THE VERY ALLY I'VE BEEN SEEKING!
WHATEVER YOU'RE LOOKIN' FOR, GORGEOUS, YOU CAN BET YOUR BOTTOM DOLLAR... I'M IT!
THUS, SMITTEN BY THE BLACK WIDOW'S FATAL BEAUTY, THE MAN CALLED HAWKEYE ENTERS INTO A DRAMATIC ALLIANCE WHICH IS TO CHANGE THE COURSE OF BOTH THEIR LIVES, AND IRON MAN'S AS WELL!

IN A LUXURIOUS SUBURB, JUST OUTSIDE THE CITY, THE BLACK WIDOW LEADS HAWKEYE THROUGH A LAVISHLY FURNISHED ESTATE UNTIL THEY REACH A STAIRWAY, LEADING TO A SUBTERRANEAN LABORATORY!
FOLLOW ME, HAWK-EYE!
TO THE ENDS OF THE EARTH, GORGEOUS!
IT IS FORTUNATE THAT HE IS TAKEN WITH MY BEAUTY! I WILL BE ABLE TO TWIST HIM AROUND MY LITTLE FINGER! BUT HE MUST NOT LEARN THAT I AM REALLY A RED SPY!

SAY! THIS IS SOME GREAT LAB YOU'VE GOT HERE! BUT YOU DON'T LOOK LIKE THE SCIENTIST TYPE TO ME!
I'M NOT! THIS EQUIPMENT BELONGS TO THE ONE I RENT THIS HOME FROM! BUT THERE ARE THINGS HERE WHICH WILL INCREASE YOUR OWN POWERS!
MY COMMUNIST MASTERS PROVIDED THIS ESTATE FOR ME! AND NOW THEIR INVESTMENT SHALL REALLY PAY OFF!

MM... I SEE WHAT YOU MEAN! SOME OF THE DEVICES DESCRIBED IN THIS BOOK WOULD MAKE GREAT WEAPONS IF FITTED ONTO MY ARROWS!
BUT WHAT'S THE ANGLE, BEAUTIFUL? DO YOU HAVE ANY DRAGONS YOU WANT SLAIN, OR WHAT??

IN A WAY, YES!! THE FAMOUS IRON MAN IS A MORTAL ENEMY OF MINE! ANY MAN WHO COULD DEFEAT HIM WOULD BE A MAN I COULD LEARN TO LOVE!
HE'S AS GOOD AS BEATEN, BABY!
BUT, ONE THING MORE... NO HARM MUST COME TO HIS EMPLOYER, TONY STARK!
SO! SHE'S GOT A CRUSH ON STARK, EH? WELL... I'LL PUT A STOP TO THAT!!

MEANTIME, THE MAN IN QUESTION IS NOW BACK AT HIS SPRAWLING FACTORY, LITTLE DREAMING OF THE DANGER THAT AWAITS HIM...
POOR PEPPER! I'M AFRAID I DIDN'T SHOW HER A VERY GOOD TIME LAST NIGHT!
I GUESS THE LEAST I CAN DO IS TAKE HER OUT AGAIN... AND THIS TIME GIVE HER THE TYPE OF GLAMOROUS EVENING SHE MUST HAVE EXPECTED!
I'LL DO IT! I'LL ASK HER RIGHT NOW!

IN FACT, I MIGHT AS WELL BE HONEST WITH MYSELF! I'M NOT DOING IT ONLY FOR HER! I'D LOVE TO TAKE THAT FABU-LOUS FEMALE TO ALL THE BEST PLACES... TO LOOK INTO THOSE GOR-GEOUS LIMPID EYES OF HERS...
CAREFUL, STARK, OL' BOY! YOU'RE BEGINNING TO SOUND LIKE A FELLA IN LOVE!

OOPS! ALMOST FORGOT! CAN'T LET HER SEE ME LIKE THIS!

MINUTES LATER...
PEPPER, THEY'VE GOT A GREAT NEW MURDER MYSTERY AT THE DRIVE-IN TONIGHT, AND I WAS WONDERIN'...?
HMM! LOOKS LIKE I'M A LITTLE LATE!
WHY, HAPPY HOGAN! YOU BIG SPEND-THRIFT, YOU!

OH! MR. STARK JUST CAME IN! I'LL SHOW HIM HE'S NOT THE ONLY FISH IN THE SEA! EVEN A MURDER MYSTERY WOULD BE BETTER THAN OUR DATE LAST NIGHT!
WELL, IF YOU DON'T WANNA...
WHO SAID I DIDN'T WANT TO ?!

I'D BE DELIGHTED TO GO TO THE DRIVE-IN MOVIE WITH YOU TONIGHT, HAPPY! IT'S CERTAINLY MORE ROMANTIC THAN BEING WALKED ALL OVER CONEY ISLAND WITH AN ICE CREAM CONE!
GRRREAT! I KNEW YOU COULDN'T RESIST MY CHARM MUCH LONGER!
WELL, I GUESS I DESERVED THAT!

MEANWHILE, A SHORT DISTANCE AWAY FROM STARK'S FACTORY...
NOW!

BULLSEYE! MY SILENT SUCTION-TIPPED ARROW WILL GET ME INSIDE STARK'S FACTORY IN SECONDS!

THIS IS ALMOST TOO EASY FOR HAWKEYE, THE MARKSMAN!
NX 8

HI, CHARLIE! SEE THE BIG GAME ON T.V. LAST NIGHT?
YOU BET! A NO-HITTER...HOW ABOUT THAT?
LET'S GO, PETE! THEY'RE WAITING FOR THAT LOAD OF EQUIPMENT INSIDE!

THEN, ONCE THE SUPPLY TRUCK HAS PASSED THROUGH THE GUARDED ENTRANCE GATE...
SO FAR, SO GOOD! NOW I'LL START ENOUGH OF A RUCKUS TO BRING IRON MAN ON THE RUN!

THE DOOR TO THE MAIN PART OF THE FACTORY IS LOCKED AND BOLTED! SO I'LL JUST SHOW THEM THAT LOCKS MEAN NOTHING TO HAWKEYE THE MARKSMAN!

THWOCK!
THAT EXPLOSIVE ARROW-HEAD WHICH THE BLACK WIDOW HELPED ME RIG UP WORKS EVEN BETTER THAN WE THOUGHT!

BUT, BEFORE THE ECHO OF THE EXPLOSION HAS DIED AWAY, A JET-POWERED AVENGING IRON MAN STREAKS TO THE SCENE, SHOUTING A BRISK COMMAND TO THE FACTORY GUARDS WHO VAINLY TRY TO MATCH HIS BLAZING SPEED...
STAY BEHIND ME, MEN! IF THERE'S ANY DANGER, I'LL FACE IT FIRST!
STAY BEHIND?? WE COULDN'T CATCH THAT IRON WHIRL-WIND IF WE TRIED!

HERE HE COMES! THIS IS ALMOST LIKE SOME CORNY FAIRY TALE! ONCE I'VE POLISHED OFF THE BIG BAD IRON MAN, I'LL RETURN TO CLAIM THE FAIR DAMSEL'S HAND!

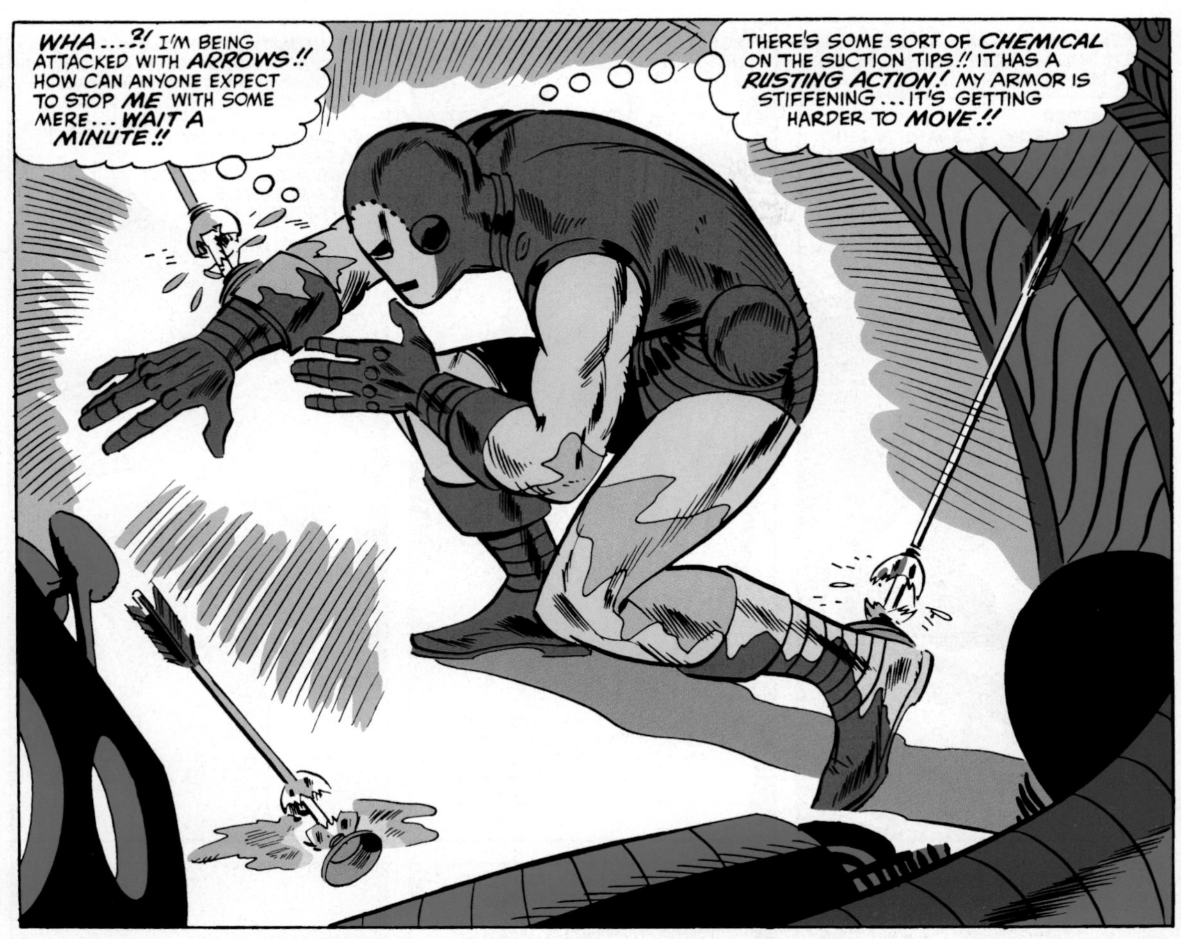
WHA...?! I'M BEING ATTACKED WITH ARROWS!! HOW CAN ANYONE EXPECT TO STOP ME WITH SOME MERE... WAIT A MINUTE!!
THERE'S SOME SORT OF CHEMICAL ON THE SUCTION TIPS!! IT HAS A RUSTING ACTION! MY ARMOR IS STIFFENING... IT'S GETTING HARDER TO MOVE!!

WHOEVER IS RESPONSIBLE HAS FOUND MY WEAK POINT! I CAN'T FIGHT RUST!!
I'VE GOT TO GET AWAY... SHED MY ARMOR BEFORE IT'S TOO RUSTY TO REMOVE!

RUNNING WON'T HELP YOU, IRON MAN! I KNOW YOU'RE HERE SOMEWHERE! YOU CAN'T ESCAPE HAWKEYE, THE MARKSMAN!!
SO THAT'S MY MYSTERIOUS ATTACKER!! WELL, HE GETS THE FIRST ROUND, BUT THE FIGHT ISN'T OVER YET! NO ONE TAKES ME BY SURPRISE TWICE!

BY THE TIME HAWKEYE REACHES THE SPOT WHERE IRON MAN HAD BEEN, ALL HE FINDS ARE ...
DISCARDED PIECES OF IRON MAN'S ARMOR! I'LL BRING THEM TO MY LAB AND ANALYZE THEM!
THE MAN WHO LEARNS ALL THE SECRETS OF IRON MAN'S ARMOR COULD BECOME ONE OF THE WORLD'S MOST POWERFUL MEN!

WHILE, IN ANOTHER SECTION OF THE SPRAWLING PLANT...
THIS IS WHAT I'M AFTER!
I'M GLAD I HAD THE FORE-SIGHT TO CONCEAL DUPLI-CATE SUITS OF ARMOR FOR MYSELF IN VARIOUS PARTS OF THE FACTORY!

MOVING WITH INCREDIBLE SPEED, LIKE A MAN POSSESSED, A FIGHTING-MAD TONY STARK DONS HIS AWE-SOME ARMOR ... EXCEPT FOR ...
MY RIGHT BOOT ASSEMBLY! IT'S MISSING!! I'D BE TOO VULNERABLE WITHOUT IT!!
I MUST FIND IT, BEFORE HAWKEYE FINDS ME!

FRANTICALLY HE SEARCHES NEAR-BY AREAS, UNTIL HE REMEMBERS...
OF COURSE! IT NEEDED REPLATING! I LEFT IT HERE AFTER IT WAS FINISHED, WAITING TILL EVERY-ONE WAS GONE BE-FORE I'D TAKE IT!

THAT DOES IT! NOW, I'VE GOT TO GO AFTER THE MARKSMAN BEFORE HE GETS TOO BIG A HEAD START! I HEARD A CAR SPEED AWAY JUST ABOUT TWO MINUTES AGO!

I HAD WONDERED HOW I'D SPEND THE EVENING WHILE PEPPER AND HAPPY WERE AT THE MOVIES! IT LOOKS AS THOUGH FATE SOLVED THAT LITTLE PROBLEM FOR ME!

THERE'S ONLY ONE CAR ON THE ROAD AT THIS HOUR, RACING AWAY FROM MY FACTORY! THAT MUST BE HAWKEYE, HEADING TOWARDS LA GUARDIA AIRPORT!
WHO CAN HE BE? WHERE DID HE COME FROM?? IT SEEMS THAT EVERY MASKED, UNUSUAL CRIMINAL IN THE EAST TRIES TO ATTACK MY WEAPONS FACTORY SOONER OR LATER! EVERY TIME I TURN AROUND I'M MENACED BY SOME CRACKPOT OR SPY!

WELL, THE FIRST THING TO DO IS STOP HIS CAR!
ZZTTTT!

...AND AN INTENSIFIED BLAST FROM MY POWER RAY IS JUST THE THING TO DO IT!!
CRASH!

IT'S HIM AGAIN! CAN THERE BE TWO IRON MEN??!
I'M ALL OUT OF RUSTING-FLUID! BUT I'VE PLENTY OF OTHER KINDS OF ARROWS FOR HIM!

BUT THIS TIME, IRON MAN IS READY FOR THE MARKSMAN'S ATTACK...
ONE OF THE HANDIEST WEAPONS OF ALL IS MY LITTLE MAGNETIC REPULSER!
13.

BUT MY TRANSISTORS WON'T POWER THE REPULSER BEAM FOREVER! I'VE GOT TO TRY A SURPRISE ATTACK OF MY OWN!
I'LL BEAT HIM SOME-HOW! I CAN'T FAIL THE GORGEOUS BLACK WIDOW!
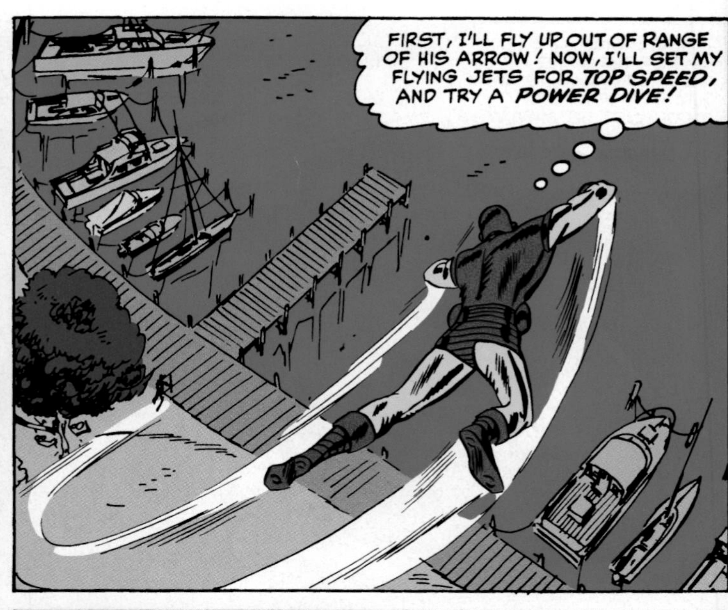
FIRST, I'LL FLY UP OUT OF RANGE OF HIS ARROW! NOW, I'LL SET MY FLYING JETS FOR TOP SPEED, AND TRY A POWER DIVE!

IT WON'T WORK! HE'S FASTER THAN I THOUGHT! HE'S PRE-PARING TO SHOOT A DIFFERENT TYPE OF ARROW AT ME!! BUT WHAT KIND IS IT??

NOW I'VE GOT YOU!!
STRONG NYLON ROPE STRANDS!! TANGLING ME UP!! CAN'T REPULSE THEM IN TIME!!
14.

BUT, NOT FOR NOTHING IS IRON MAN'S MIGHT SPOKEN OF IN HUSHED TONES BY THE UNDERWORLD! WITH AN IRRESISTIBLE SURGE OF POWER, HIS TRANSISTOR-AIDED MUSCLES FLING HIS ARMS APART, THUS SNAPPING THE STRANDS BEFORE THEY CAN TIGHTEN!

HE BROKE FREE!! WHAT'S HE TRYING NOW??
I'VE GOT TO HIT THE PIER WITH JUST ENOUGH FORCE!

I DID IT!
WHAM!
RIP!

WHAT GOT INTO HIM?? HE'S LIKE AN AVENGING TORNADO!!

LOOK OUT! STOP! WHAT ARE YOU DOING?!!
JUST TRYING TO KEEP YOU FROM GETTING BORED, ROBIN HOOD!

TWANNG!

OH, NO YOU DON'T!! YOU CAN'T ESCAPE ME BY DROWNING! YOU'VE GOT TOO MUCH EXPLAINING TO DO!!

BUT A PAIR OF THE MOST GLAMOROUS EYES IN THE WORLD ARE ALSO WATCHING THE GRIM TABLEAU FROM A HIDING PLACE NEARBY...
I WAS TO PICK HIM UP HERE AFTER HIS VICTORY... A VICTORY WHICH NEVER TOOK PLACE!!

BUT THEN, THINKING THE BATTLE WON, THE GOLDEN AVENGER MAKES HIS MOST SERIOUS MISTAKE... TURNING HIS BACK ON HAWKEYE...
WHILE HE'S UNCONSCIOUS, I'LL GO TO HIS CAR AND RETRIEVE THE PIECES OF MY OTHER SUIT OF ARMOR!
15.

---AS THE MUFFLED PADDING OF IRON MAN'S HEAVY FEET FADES AWAY...
HE'S GONE!!

NOW IS MY CHANCE TO FINISH HIM OFF FOR GOOD!

NOW, WHEN HE LEAST EXPECTS IT!

I'LL USE MY MOST POTENT ARROW OF ALL...!!

...THE DEMOLITION BLAST WARHEAD WHICH THE BLACK WIDOW HELPED ME TO ASSEMBLE!!

AND NOW... FAREWELL, IRON MAN!! NOTHING CAN SAVE YOU NOW!

But, Hawkeye is *wrong!* There is one thing that *can* save Iron Man... and that is the protection of the strongest, most skillfully made flexible iron armor in existence, tempered to the highest degree of resiliency ever attained by any metal!
WHOOM!
And, although the demolition blast ricochets harmlessly off the shoulder of the golden avenger, the tremendous impact is hurled away in another direction.. right towards the startled *Madame Natasha*, before she can save herself!

OHHH!
HAWKEYE!! SAVE ME!

YOU!! WHAT HAVE I DONE?!

Ignoring the stunned Iron Man, the anguished marksman races to the side of the Black Widow!
SHE'S STILL BREATHING! I CAN'T LET HER DIE!!

HER BOAT IS WAITING! IF I CAN JUST MAKE IT TO A DOCTOR WITH HER BEFORE THE FOG ROLLS IN...!
SHE HAS TO LIVE!! SHE HAS TO BE *MINE!!* SHE'S THE ONLY ONE I'VE EVER LOVED!!

NOTE: FOR THE THRILLING "ORIGIN OF IRON MAN" DON'T MISS "MARVEL TALES ANNUAL"... NOW ON SALE!

CONTINUED IN *MARVEL MASTERWORKS: THE INVINCIBLE IRON MAN VOL. 2.*

CAPT.
AMERICA
15¢
IND
117
SEPT
MARVEL
COMICS
GROUP
APPROVED
BY THE
COMICS
CODE
AUTHORITY
CAPTAIN AMERICA
THE COMING OF THE FALCON!

CAPTAIN AMERICA, LIVING LEGEND of WORLD WAR II TM
THE COMING OF... THE FALCON!
SO FAR, THE REAL CAPTAIN AMERICA, TRAPPED WITHIN THE RED SKULL'S BODY, HAS MANAGED TO SURVIVE MY EVERY TRAP! BUT THIS TIME HE IS DOOMED---AS I SEND HIM TO THE ISLE WHERE THOSE WHO HATE ME MOST AWAIT THEIR DAY OF VENGEANCE! THE ISLE OF---
THE EXILES!
THE RED SKULL... THRU THE POWER OF HIS COSMIC CUBE---IS HURLING ME THRU SPACE ---TO WHERE?
STORY and ART:
STAN (THE MAN) LEE
and
GENE (THE DEAN) COLAN
JOE SINNOTT, EMBELLISHER
SAM ROSEN, LETTERER

AN ISLAND... LONELY AND DESOLATE... SOMEWHERE IN THE TROPICS!
IT MUST BE ONE OF THE MANY REMOTE AREAS WHERE THE SKULL HAS HIDDEN BASES!

EVEN AS I LAND HERE... I CAN ALMOST FEEL HIS EYES UPON ME...
HE'S WATCHING... SCHEMING... REVELLING IN MY HELPLESS-NESS!

BUT LET THE MADMAN GLOAT... WHILE HE CAN!
SOONER OR LATER, HE'S BOUND TO MAKE A SLIP...
AND WHEN HE DOES... I'LL BE READY AND WAITING ...TO STRIKE BACK!

HE HASN'T YET LOST FAITH! WHY CAN'T I CRUSH HIS SPIRIT?
BUT, NO MATTER! NOT EVEN HIS INDOMITABLE WILL CAN SAVE HIM NOW!

NOTHING CAN SAVE HIM... FROM THOSE WHO ARE COMING!

I HEAR VOICES... COMING CLOSER... IN THE DISTANCE!

THE ACCURSED SKULL THOUGHT HE HAD SEEN THE LAST OF US WHEN HE MAROONED US UPON THIS BARREN ISLE!
BUT SOON WE SHALL BE FREE OF THIS WRETCHED PLACE ---FREE TO SEEK OUR DEADLY REVENGE!
THERE IS NO PLACE ON EARTH WHERE HE CAN HIDE FROM US!
NO PLACE ON EARTH WHERE HE CAN BE SAFE ... WHERE THE SKULL CAN ESCAPE THE COMBINED POWER OF ---THE EXILES!

IT WAS WE WHO FOUND THE ALL-MIGHTY COSMIC CUBE!
IT IS WE WHO MUST SHARE ITS SUPREME, EARTH-SHATTERING POWER!
AND SHARE IT WE SHALL, CADAVUS! SO WE HAVE SWORN!
THE SKULL WILL NOT ESCAPE US!
ONLY THE RED SKULL'S DEATH CAN GIVE US OUR TOTAL TRIUMPH!

SO THAT'S WHY HE SENT ME TO THIS SPOT!
IF THEY FIND ME... I'M DONE FOR!

THE TREE... SHAKING LOOSE FROM BENEATH ME!
IT'S MORE OF HIS DOING! HE'S STILL WATCHING! HE WILLED IT!

LOOK! FALLING FROM THE UNDERBRUSH ...AHEAD OF US...!
THEY SEE ME!
4.

IT'S HIM!! IT'S ALMOST AS THOUGH... WE WILLED IT TO HAPPEN!
TRICK OR NOT... HE WILL NEVER LEAVE HERE... ALIVE!
CAREFUL! IT MUST BE A TRICK! WHY WOULD HE COME HERE THIS WAY... ALONE... UNARMED?

NO USE EVEN TRYING TO CONVINCE THEM THAT I'M NOT THE REAL RED SKULL!
THEY'D NEVER BELIEVE IT!
SO... THERE'S NOTHING TO DO... BUT FIGHT FOR MY LIFE!
I WILL ATTACK HIM FIRST!
IT WAS YOU WHO TAUGHT ME TO MAKE A LETHAL WEAPON OF MY SCARF!
SO NOW IT IS YOUR TURN TO FEEL ITS DEADLY STING!

HE DOESN'T REALIZE THAT WE'VE BOTH FOUGHT BEFORE!
I REMEMBER BALDINI'S SKILL...AND HIS WEAKNESS!

AT THE INSTANT HIS SCARF MAKES CONTACT...
HE MUST LOOSEN HIS GRIP... FOR TOTAL MOBILITY!
AND, AT THAT VERY SPLIT-SECOND...
...I STRIKE!

I SHALL FINISH HIM...WITH A SINGLE SHOT!
NO, CHANG!
MY MURDER CHAIR WILL DO IT BETTER!

SHOOOSST!
I WAS READY FOR THAT ONE!
BUT HOW LONG CAN I KEEP DODGING HIS INEXHAUSTIBLE BLASTS?
6

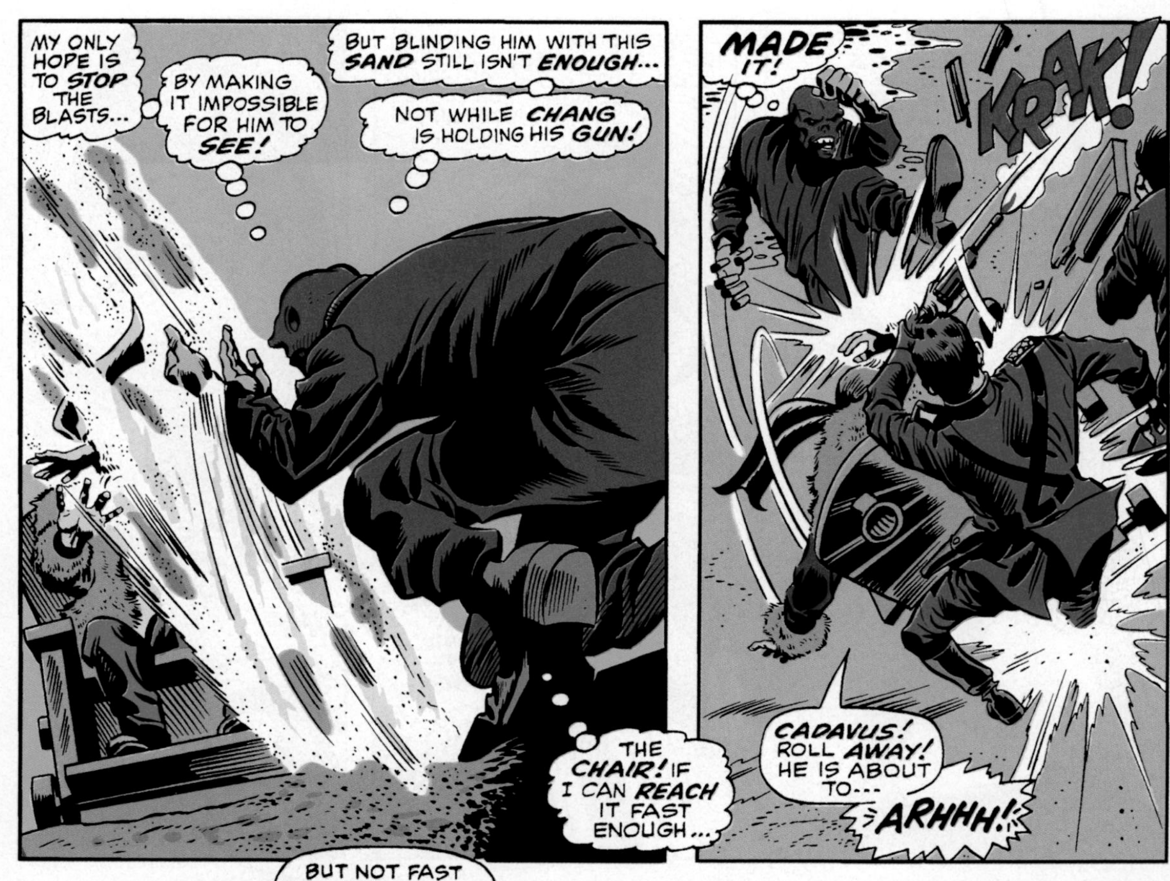
MY ONLY HOPE IS TO STOP THE BLASTS...
BY MAKING IT IMPOSSIBLE FOR HIM TO SEE!
BUT BLINDING HIM WITH THIS SAND STILL ISN'T ENOUGH...
NOT WHILE CHANG IS HOLDING HIS GUN!
THE CHAIR! IF I CAN REACH IT FAST ENOUGH...
MADE IT!
KRAK!
CADAVUS! ROLL AWAY! HE IS ABOUT TO---
ARHHH!

YOU MOVE FASTER THAN EVER, SKULL...
BUT NOT FAST ENOUGH TO EVADE ALL THE EXILES!
SNAP!
GRUNING... BEHIND ME!
WHILE, FROM THE FRONT...
NOW WE HAVE YOU...

IT WILL BE IRON-HAND HAUPTMANN WHO SLAYS THE RED SKULL!

WHAT A MAGNIFICENT STROKE OF SHEER GENIUS ON MY PART!
NOT ONLY WILL HE DIE... BUT HE WILL FALL IN THE GUISE OF HIS MOST HATED FOE!

NO NEED TO WATCH HIS FINAL MOMENTS...
SUCH SORDID SIGHTS DEPRESS ME!
AND, THERE IS STILL A WORLD FOR ME TO WIN!

BUT, EVEN AS THE REAL SKULL TURNS TRIUMPHANTLY AWAY...
HAUPTMANN... LOOK OUT!
A FALCON! IF... THOSE CLAWS HAD STRUCK MY FACE...!
HE TURNED AWAY!
IF I CAN LASH OUT FAST ENOUGH...

IT'LL TAKE MORE THAN AN IRON HAND TO SHIELD YOU FROM THIS!
YOU HAVE BEEN LUCKY, SKULL!
BUT YOUR LUCK CANNOT HOLD OUT FOREVER!
NOT AGAINST THE UNBREAKABLE GRIP OF KRUSHKI!
NO! NO! IT IS THE ACCURSED BIRD AGAIN!

WHUFF!
OKAY, KRUSHKI ...YOU'VE HAD IT!

THAT'S THE SECOND TIME THE FALCON GOT ME A BREATHER!
IT'S ALMOST AS THOUGH HE KNOWS WHAT HE'S DOING... AS THOUGH HE'S ACTING UNDER ORDERS!
NOW... IF I CAN JUST MAKE IT TO THE UNDER-BRUSH...!

HE'S LEAVING... LIKE SOMEONE WHO KNOWS THAT HIS JOB IS DONE!
BUT THEY'LL BE SEARCHING FOR ME AGAIN IN MINUTES! I STILL HAVE TO...
SAY! I JUST REALIZED SOMETHING...!
THIS GROTESQUE SKULL FACE IS REALLY JUST A MASK!
CHANCES ARE... THE EXILES HAVE NEVER EVEN SEEN THE FACE BENEATH!
SO, IF I JUST REMOVE IT...

I SHOULD HAVE THOUGHT OF THIS LONG AGO!
I WOULDN'T HAVE HAD TO WORRY ABOUT THE POLICE... OR ANYONE!
NOBODY WOULD EVER RECOGNIZE THE SKULL WITHOUT HIS MASK!
AND YET... WHAT IF THE EXILES HAVE SEEN HIS FACE!

I CAN'T AFFORD TO CHANCE IT!
BUT, IF I CAN USE THIS CLAY PROPERLY... I WON'T HAVE TO...
IT'LL FURNISH A PERFECT BASE FOR A MAKESHIFT DISGUISE!

MEANWHILE, BACK IN NEW YORK---
STARE, YOU FOOLS! STARE AT YOUR HERO, CAPTAIN AMERICA!
LITTLE DO YOU DREAM THAT MY EXILES HAVE ALREADY WRITTEN FINIS TO HIS MISERABLE CAREER!

BUT I AM NOT SOME COSTUMED ODDITY... SOME COLORFUL FREAK TO BE GAPED AT BY THE UNDESERVING MASSES!
TAXI! WAIT!
CAPTAIN AMERICA?!!
HEY, I THOUGHT YOU GUYS JUST KINDA FLEW THRU THE AIR!
THERE IS NO NEED TO THINK! JUST DRIVE!

THE GRINNING, WAVING, SIMPERING PUBLIC! HOW I DESPISE IT!
IF ONLY THEY KNEW...AS I BENIGNLY SMILE AT THEM...
THEY SOON SHALL BE MY HELPLESS SLAVES!

FOR, SO LONG AS THE COSMIC CUBE IS MINE---
THERE IS NOTHING BEYOND THE GRASP OF THE RED SKULL!
RAD CITY
KIRK DOUGLAS - BROTHERHOOD
AND IT SHALL BE MINE... FOREVER!

I HAVE NO MONEY WITH ME... BUT IF YOU WILL GIVE ME YOUR NAME AND ADDRESS...
THAT'S OKAY, CAP! IT'S A PLEASURE TO GIVE A GUY LIKE YOU A FREE RIDE! JUST FORGET IT, PAL!
PRECISELY WHAT I INTEND TO DO, YOU HERO-WORSHIPPING SIMPLETON!
LOOK! ACROSS THE STREET! IT'S CAPTAIN AMERICA!
HE MUST BE REGISTERING AT THE HOTEL! HOW ABOUT THAT!
WELL, I GUESS HE'S GOTTA BED DOWN SOMEWHERE!

STRANGE...I NEVER THOUGHT CAPTAIN AMERICA WOULD SWAGGER SO!
ALMOST AS IF HE REVELS IN THE ATTENTION OF THE PUBLIC!
CAPTAIN AMERICA! ARE YOU GOING TO BE STAYING HERE?
WHY NOT? ISN'T IT THE BEST HOTEL IN TOWN?

FEEL HIS MUSCLES, GALS! IT'LL MAKE A GREAT PIC!
OHHH!
ENJOY IT WHILE YOU MAY, MY DEAR!
FOR SOON YOU WILL BOW TO ME, INSTEAD!

CLICK!
CLICK!
CLICK!
TAKE ALL THE PICTURES YOU WISH!

FOR, LITTLE DO YOU DREAM THAT YOU ARE MERELY PERPETUATING THE SHALLOW MEMORY OF... A DEAD MAN!

I COULD OBLITERATE THEM ALL... IN LESS THAN A SECOND... MERELY BY WILLING IT!
BUT IT WOULD BE TOO SIMPLE... TOO SWIFT... TOO UNSATISFYING!
SINCE I KNOW THAT THE POWER IS MINE, I CAN AFFORD TO WAIT... TO BIDE MY TIME!
I MUST FIND THE PERFECT MOMENT!
MEANWHILE, I'LL ALLOW THEM TO FAWN OVER ME... JUST AS THE WHOLE HUMAN RACE SHALL LEARN TO DO!
THIS IS GREAT, CAP!
NOW FLEX YOUR BICEPS A LITTLE, HUH?
I DON'T GET IT! HE WAS ALWAYS CAMERA-SHY!
ANYONE CAN CHANGE! COULD BE THAT ALL THE PUBLICITY HAS GONE TO HIS HEAD!
13.

WHAT ABOUT YOUR NEW, TEENAGE SIDEKICK, CAP?
SIDEKICK? CAPTAIN AMERICA NEEDS NO SIDE-KICK!
THEN THAT WHOLE BIT WITH THE YOUNG-STER IN A BUCKY BARNES COSTUME WAS JUST A PUBLI-CITY STUNT... IS THAT IT?
SURE, SURE! CALL IT WHAT YOU WANT TO!

I'D BETTER END THIS NOW!
THE QUESTIONS ARE BECOMING TOO PERSONAL... TOO PROBING!
THAT WILL BE ALL NOW! GOOD NIGHT!

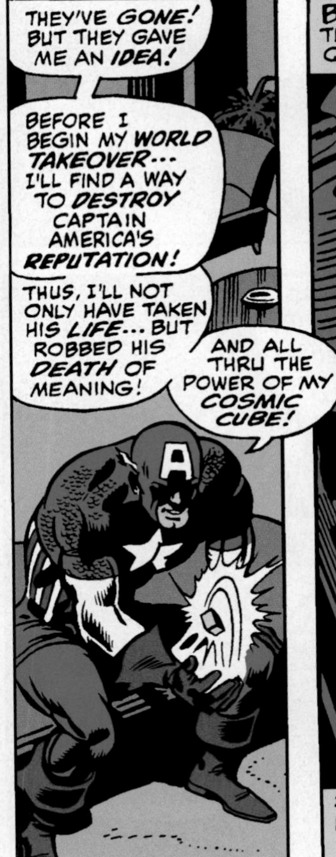
THEY'VE GONE! BUT THEY GAVE ME AN IDEA!
BEFORE I BEGIN MY WORLD TAKEOVER... I'LL FIND A WAY TO DESTROY CAPTAIN AMERICA'S REPUTATION!
THUS, I'LL NOT ONLY HAVE TAKEN HIS LIFE... BUT ROBBED HIS DEATH OF MEANING!
AND ALL THRU THE POWER OF MY COSMIC CUBE!

BUT, IS THE CUBE REALLY HIS? AT THAT VERY MOMENT, AT THE HEAD-QUARTERS OF A.I.M.,* WE FIND...
THE WORLD THOUGHT MODOK DEAD! BUT HE LIVES... TO GUIDE US ONCE AGAIN!
*ADVANCED IDEA MECHANICS... THE EVIL SECRET SOCIETY WHO CREATED THE COSMIC CUBE! ...STAN.

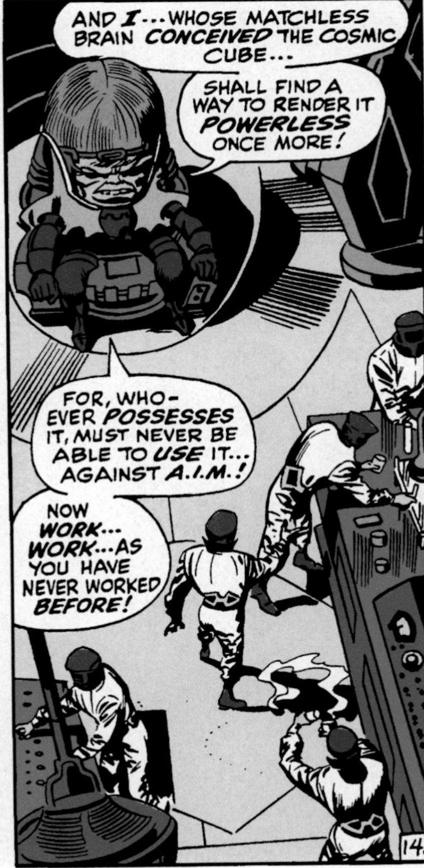
AND I... WHOSE MATCHLESS BRAIN CONCEIVED THE COSMIC CUBE...
SHALL FIND A WAY TO RENDER IT POWERLESS ONCE MORE!
FOR, WHO-EVER POSSESSES IT, MUST NEVER BE ABLE TO USE IT... AGAINST A.I.M.!
NOW WORK... WORK... AS YOU HAVE NEVER WORKED BEFORE!
14.

GOOD WORK, RED-WING! ONCE AGAIN WE'VE TAUNTED THE EXILES BY ROBBING THEM OF A VICTIM!
HOWEVER, STILL MORE SURPRISES AWAIT US, AS WE RETURN TO THE ISLE OF EXILES, TO FIND...
...EVEN THOUGH THAT JOKER IN THE RED JUMP-SUIT LOOKED AS THOUGH HE MIGHT HAVE TAKEN THEM BY HIMSELF!

BUT NOW, WE'D BETTER RETURN TO THE VILLAGE!
IF THE EXILES EVER CATCH US, THEY MAY NOT APPRECIATE OUR LITTLE GAMES!
MEANWHILE, JUST A FEW YARDS AWAY...

THERE! LEARNING HOW TO CHANGE MY FEATURES WITH CLAY HAD SAVED MY LIFE MANY TIMES DURING WORLD WAR TWO...
BUT I NEVER EXPECTED TO DO IT AGAIN, TWO DECADES LATER, IN A BODY NOT MY OWN!

I HOPE I DIDN'T MAKE THE CRUDE DISGUISE RESEMBLE MY OWN NATURAL FEATURES TOO MUCH!
WELL, AT LEAST I MADE THE HAIR MUCH DARKER!
UH OH! SOMEONE'S COMING! --BUT IT'S NOT THE EXILES!
A MAN WITH A FALCON---THE VERY BIRD THAT SAVED ME!
HEY! HOLD IT! I WANT TO TALK TO YOU!
WHO ARE YOU, MISTER? HOW'D YOU GET ON THIS ISLAND?
IT'S OKAY, REDWING! HE'S NOT ONE OF THEM!
YOU WOULDN'T BELIEVE ME IF I TOLD YOU!
BUT I'M MIGHTY GRATEFUL TO YOU AND THAT SHARP-CLAWED PET OF YOURS!

THEN YOU'RE THE ONE IN THAT SCARLET GETUP WHO WAS FIGHTING THE EXILES!
ANY ENEMY OF THEIRS IS A FULL-TIME FRIEND OF MINE!
THAT GOES DOUBLE FOR ME, PAL!
...SPECIALLY SINCE YOU SOUND MORE HARLEM THAN HAITIAN!

YOU KNOW IT, MAN! I'M A BIG CITY BROTHER FROM WAY BACK!
NOW, FOLLOW ME... BEFORE THE EXILES FIND US!

MINUTES LATER---
THIS USED TO BE A HAPPY VILLAGE... UNTIL THE EXILES CAME!
THE NATIVES WERE PEACEFUL --- DIDN'T EVEN HAVE A POPGUN BETWEEN THEM...
SO IT WASN'T LONG BEFORE THEY WERE TURNED INTO SERFS BY THEIR NEW, WELL-ARMED MASTERS!

I'VE BEEN TRYING TO ORGANIZE THEM... BAND THEM TOGETHER AND GET THEM TO FIGHT FOR THE FREE-DOM THAT THEY'VE LOST!
BUT, IT'S AN UP-HILL JOB!
IT WOULD HAVE, TO BE!
THE EXILES ARE PROFESSIONAL KILLERS!

BUT WHAT ABOUT YOU? WHO ARE YOU? WHAT'S YOUR STAKE IN ALL THIS?
I'VE BEEN WONDERING ABOUT THAT MYSELF! IT'S KINDA FUNNY HOW IT ALL HAPPENED...
EVER SINCE I CAN REMEMBER, I'VE BEEN NUTS ABOUT BIRDS!
I USED TO HAVE THE BIGGEST PIGEON COOP ON ANY ROOFTOP IN HARLEM!
MAN! I COULD PRACTICALLY MAKE THOSE HIGH-FLYERS TALK!
BUT THEN... I GOT ALL HUNG UP ON FALCONS..!

"IT STARTED IN RIO... WHERE I WENT FOR A VACATION..."
"THE FIRST TIME I SAW ONE... I WAS HOOKED... BUT FOR GOOD!"

"THEN, I FINALLY FOUND REDWING... AND BOUGHT HIM FOR MY OWN!"
"WE'VE GOT SOMETHING GOIN' FOR US THAT NOBODY ELSE COULD UNDERSTAND--!"

"HE'S MORE THAN A BIRD! MORE THAN A FALCON! IT'S LIKE... HE'S A PART OF ME!"

WELL, TO MAKE A LONG STORY SHORT, I ANSWERED AN AD IN THE PAPER...
IT WAS FROM THE EXILES... BUT I DIDN'T KNOW THEM AT THE TIME!
THEY WERE BORED... LOOKING FOR KICKS! THEY WANTED TO HIRE A HUNTING FALCON!
SO, REDWING AND ME HOPPED THE FIRST FREIGHTER ...AND HERE WE ARE!

BUT, WHEN I SAW WHAT A SUCKER PLAY I'D MADE... WE CUT OUT... BUT FAST!
THE EXILES DON'T HIRE WORKERS...
THEY JUST KEEP PRISONERS!
YOU SAID SOMETHING BEFORE ...ABOUT ORGANIZING THE OTHERS HERE... TO FIGHT BACK...!

HOW DO YOU PLAN TO DO IT, WITHOUT ANY WEAPONS?
WE'LL MAKE WEAPONS! OUT OF STICKS 'N STONES IF WE HAVE TO!
ANY-THING'S BETTER THAN NOT FIGHTING BACK!
AFTER THE WAY I SAW YOU HANDLE YOURSELF BACK THERE...
I'M KINDA HOPING YOU'LL TOSS IN WITH ME!

YOU COULDN'T STOP ME, FRIEND!
BUT IT'LL TAKE MORE THAN GUTS! THEY'VE GOT THE ARMS... YOU'LL NEED A GIMMICK!
YEAH? LIKE WHAT?
I THINK I'VE GOT IT..!

YOU NEED SOME-THING TO SERVE AS A SYMBOL TO THE NATIVES...
AND SOMETHING THAT'LL UNNERVE THE EXILES... MAKE THEM WONDER WHO THEY'RE FIGHTING!
A MASK AND COSTUME OUGHT TO DO IT... TOGETHER WITH A STIRRING NAME... LIKE, FOR INSTANCE... THE FALCON!
ME, A COSTUMED CLOWN?
DON'T PUT ME ON, MAN!
DON'T KNOCK IT, FELLA! IT'S BEEN KNOWN TO WORK!
AND I'M THE GUY TO SHOW YOU HOW!
19

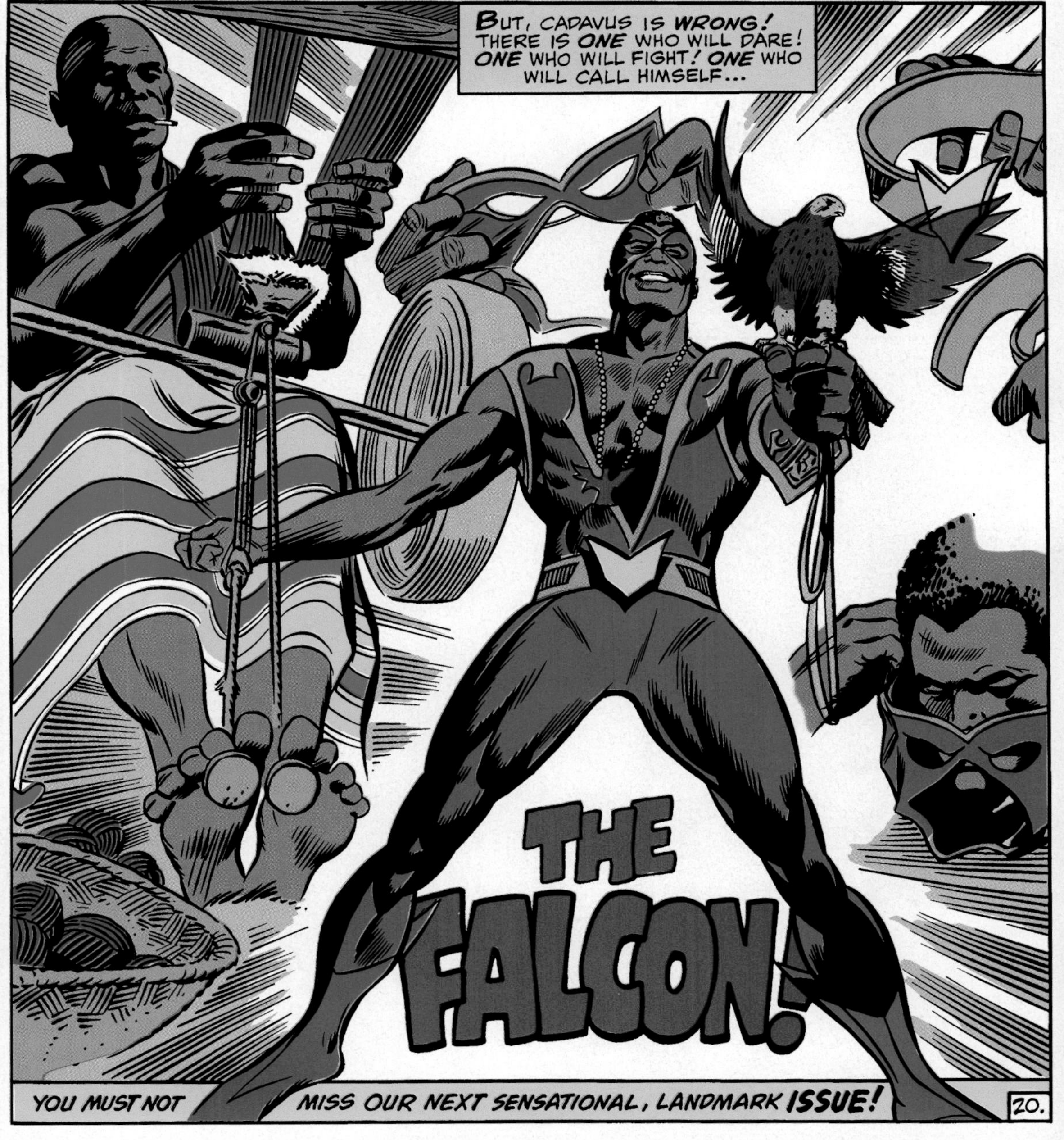

CONTINUED IN *MARVEL MASTERWORKS: CAPTAIN AMERICA VOL. 4.*

CAPTAIN AMERICA
OUT OF TIME
PART 6
EPTING after Sanjulian
fgd

During the dark days of the early 1940s, a covert military experiment turned Steve Rogers into America's first Super-Soldier, CAPTAIN AMERICA.

Throughout the war, Cap and his partner Bucky fought alongside our infantry and with a group of heroes known as the Invaders. In the closing months of WWII, Captain America and Bucky were both presumed dead in an explosion over the Arctic Ocean.

Decades later, a figure was found trapped in ice, and Captain America was revived. Having slept through more than half of the 20th century, Steve Rogers awakened to a world he never imagined, a world where war had moved from the battlefield to the city streets... A world in dire need of...

CAPTAIN AMERICA

OUT OF TIME Part 6

Aleksander Lukin, a rogue Soviet general, uses a cybernetic assassin to kill the Red Skull and steal from him a slightly damaged Cosmic Cube. Then, Lukin's men in London seize one of the Skull's Weapons of Mass Destruction, which was designed to help charge the Cube. In the midst of this chaos, Captain America's mind has begun to play tricks on him. Old and confusing memories continue to resurface, almost as if he were under a mental attack.

As clues begin to pile up, Cap and S.H.I.E.L.D. director Nick Fury come to suspect that Lukin, who is now publicly known as the head of an international corporation, is the man behind it all, and that the seeds of his vendetta may lie in an Invaders mission from decades past.

Cap leaves Fury to investigate further while he tries to get to the bottom of the mysterious memories that have been plaguing him. But Fury is keeping something from Cap, something he fears could destroy him.

Writer
Ed Brubaker

Artist
Steve Epting

Colorist
Frank D'Armata

Letterer
VC's Randy Gentile

Production
Jacob Chabot

Assistant Editors
Schmidt, Moore & Lazer

Editor
Tom Brevoort

Editor in Chief
Joe Quesada

Publisher
Dan Buckley

Captain America created by Joe Simon & Jack Kirby

Somewhere Beneath Philadelphia
YES, SIR... WE'LL BE IN PLACE WITHIN THE HOUR, GENERAL LUKIN.
THE DEVICE IS SET TO THE REMOTE...
...AND THE SCAPEGOAT IS IN POSITION.
IF ALL GOES ACCORDING TO PLAN, YOU SHOULD HAVE PLAUSIBLE DENIABILITY ON EVERYTHING THAT HAPPENS TODAY.
WERE YOU ABLE TO GET THE RECEPTOR SET UP?
THAT'S GOOD...HUNH-HUH.
ENOUGH ENERGY LEFT FOR WHAT?

NO, YOU'RE RIGHT, SIR, THAT IS NONE OF MY CONCERN... EXCUSE ME.
YES, SIR...I AM...I'M ABOUT TO TAKE CARE OF THE S.H.I.E.L.D. WOMAN RIGHT NOW. EXACTLY AS ORDERED...

S.H.I.E.L.D. Helicarrier--
HEADQUARTERS OF THE U.N. PEACEKEEPING TASKFORCE
--'COURSE I KNOW. I'M THE ONE WHO SENT HER OUT THERE.
SURE, BUT WHAT THE HELL'RE YOU DOING ABOUT IT?
WHAT I HEAR, SHE HASN'T REPORTED IN FOR OVER TWENTY-FOUR HOURS. THAT'S NOT LIKE SHARON AND YOU KNOW IT.
YOU WANNA TAKE THAT TONE DOWN A NOTCH AND ADD A "SIR" AT THE END, AGENT TAPPER?
SORRY... SIR...
IT'S JUST, SHARON, UH... AGENT 13 AND I...WE...
I KNOW. BUT I THOUGHT THAT WAS OVER, NEAL?

THAT WAS MY MISTAKE... I DIDN'T WANT HER TAKING THE LIAISON GIG WITH ROGERS. JEALOUS, I GUESS, WITH THEIR HISTORY AND ALL.
SO I TRIED TO PUT MY FOOT DOWN, BUT... WELL...

SHARON PUT HER FOOT WHERE THE SUN DON'T SHINE.
BASICALLY.
SHE'S TOUGH AS NAILS, THAT GIRL. WHICH IS WHY I'M TRYING NOT TO WORRY, YET.

LOOK, I'VE GOT TEAMS SWEEPING PHILLY RIGHT NOW, AND OUR SATELLITES ARE SCANNING THE ENTIRE EASTERN SEABOARD FOR A SIGNAL FROM HER COMMUNICATOR.
IF IT'LL MAKE YOU FEEL ANY BETTER, YOU CAN JOIN THE EFFORT.
THAT WOULD HELP, SIR, YEAH...I JUST...I CAN'T SIT AROUND HERE DOING NOTHING.

UNDERSTOOD, AGENT. TAKE A CAR DOWN... BUT NOT ONE OF MY PORSCHES.
I'LL HAVE ONE OF THE TEAM LEADERS RADIO YOU WITH THEIR 20.

IS HE DOWN THERE... LOOKING FOR HER?
CAPTAIN AMERICA?
YES, SIR.
NO. HE'S GOT ENOUGH ON HIS MIND RIGHT NOW AS IT IS.

HE DOESN'T EVEN KNOW SHE'S MISSING, AND I'D LIKE TO FIND HER BEFORE HE HAS TO BE TOLD...

BULLETS ARE REAL ENOUGH.
WHATEVER'S GOING ON HERE, ONE THING'S CLEAR...
...I'VE GOTTA GET OUT--NOW!
KRAK!
KRAK!
KRAK!
DDABUDDABUDDABUDDABUDDABUDDABUDDABUDD

SKRASHH!

KRAK!
KRAK!

OF COURSE...

...THEY'RE ALL GONE.
NO EVIDENCE THEY WERE REALLY HERE AT ALL.

BUT THEY WERE. I CAN STILL SMELL THE GUNFIRE IN THE AIR.
ALL OF THIS-- THESE UNLOCKED MEMORIES, THE STRANGE DREAMS, AND NOW THESE VANISHING NAZIS-- IT'S ALL THE CUBE. IT HAS TO BE.
WHOEVER'S GOT IT, LUKIN OR WHOEVER ELSE...THEY'RE MANIPULATING ME.
BUT TO WHAT PURPOSE? WHY WOULD SOMEONE WANT ME...
...HERE?
I CAN MAKE IT, CAP! I CAN MAKE IT!
BUCKY, WAIT!
GOT IT!

WAIT! IT'S PROBABLY BOOBY-TRAPPED!
I SEE IT! AW GOD, CAP, IT'S GONNA BLOW!
NO! I'M LOSING MY GRIP!
DROP OFF, BUCKY!
LET GO!
I CAN'T!
I'M STUCK!

...OH GOD... HE COULDN'T LET GO...

WHAT DOES THIS MEAN? IS IT EVEN REAL? ARE ANY OF THESE MEMORIES REAL?
WHY DO I FEEL SO SURE THEY ARE?

SOMETHING FURY SAID... ABOUT THE COSMIC CUBE STILL NEEDING TO BE CHARGED. THAT'S WHAT THE SKULL'S W.M.D.S WERE FOR...TO CONVERT DEATH INTO ENERGY.

WHICH MEANS THE CUBE THE SKULL HAD WHEN HE DIED IS WEAK.

BUT MAYBE IT'S JUST POWERFUL ENOUGH TO UNLOCK THESE MEMORIES INSIDE ME AND MAKE ME FIGHT PHANTOMS...
...TO GIVE ME BACK JUST ENOUGH OF MY PAST TO TORTURE ME.

YOU FIND WHAT YOU WERE LOOKING FOR UP THERE, SIR?
I FOUND SOMETHING... I'M JUST NOT SURE WHAT.

SO, BACK TO THE HELICARRIER, THEN?
SURE, WHY DON'T YOU--

UNH!
HEY! YOU--

--OKAY?
...SHARON...

WE'VE GOT TO GET BACK TO THE STATES, *NOW!* HOW *FAST* CAN THIS THING GO?

YOU KNOW THE *CONCORDE?*
YES.

WELL, COMPARED TO OUR *TOP SPEED,* THE CONCORDE'S LIKE *WALKING.*
TOP SPEED THEN.

S.H.I.E.L.D. Helicarrier--
COLONEL FURY'S PRIVATE OFFICE-- THIRTY MINUTES LATER
COLONEL, STEVE ROGERS IS ON SECURE ONE.
RIGHT, TERESA, PUT HIM THROUGH.
FURY HERE, WHAT'S--
SHARON'S BEEN CAPTURED.
I KNOW... I'VE GOT TEAMS COMBING THE STREETS FOR HER AS WE SPEAK.
DAMN IT, FURY, YOU SHOULD'VE TOLD ME.
NO. SOMEONE'S PULLING OUR STRINGS, ROGERS. EVER THINK THAT IT MIGHT BE EXACTLY WHAT THEY WANT, FOR YOU TO GO RUSHING IN BLIND?
I KNOW THEY DO...THEY SHOWED ME EXACTLY WHERE TO FIND HER.
WHAT? WHY THE HELL DIDN'T YOU SAY SO?
I CAN HAVE TEAMS IN PLACE IN TWO MINUTES. WHERE IS--
SORRY, NICK, I'D HAVE RADIOED IN EARLIER...BUT COMMUNICATIONS WERE OFFLINE AT TOP SPEED...
...ANYWAY, I'M HERE NOW. I'LL TAKE CARE OF IT.
WAIT, CAP--THERE'S SOMETHING YOU NEED TO KNOW...
NO TIME, NICK--

--I'VE GOT A VISUAL. ROGERS OUT.
SNAKT

YEEEAAAAAAA!
RATATATATAT

WAP

HOLD ON, I GOT YOU... YOU'RE OKAY NOW.

STEVE--OH GOD, IT'S A SET-UP!
I'M SURE IT IS, LET'S JUST GET THESE CHAINS OFF OF YOU AND WE'LL DEAL WITH IT.

YOU DON'T UNDERSTAND, STEVE. THE GUY WE'VE BEEN HUNTING--THE MAN WHO KILLED THE RED SKULL--
--I'VE SEEN HIM!

"--I THINK--
I THINK IT'S BUCKY!"
THEY'RE IN POSITION, GENERAL.
SHOULD I TAKE THE SHOT?
NO. REGARDLESS OF YOUR PERSONAL FEELINGS, THAT IS NOT THE PLAN.
IT'S NOT ABOUT FEELINGS, SIR, THE MAN IS SIMPLY GOOD. HE'S GOING TO BE A PROBLEM.
I'M SURE HE WILL BE. BUT HE'LL SUFFER MUCH MORE BEFORE HE BECOMES OUR PROBLEM...

...AND THEN YOU'LL GET TO DEAL WITH HIM.
JUST COMPLETE THE MISSION. WE BROUGHT HIM HERE FOR A REASON, AFTER ALL.
YES, SIR, GENERAL LUKIN. CONSIDER IT DONE.

DEET

...DAMN IT...HOW COULD THEY HAVE MISSED THIS ALL THOSE YEARS?

COLONEL? ONE OF THE PHILADELPHIA TEAMS HAS FOUND SOMETHING...
BERLIN
DULLES INTERNATIONAL NOV 2004

THIS IS FURY, GO.
AGENT TAPPER HERE, SIR. GOT A BIG PROBLEM...WE MANAGED TO TRACK AGENT 13'S COMMUNICATOR--

--BUT THERE'S A BODY HERE. AND SOME KIND OF BOMB LIKE THE ONE IN YESTERDAY'S BRIEFING.
GET OUTTA THERE, TAPPER. NOW!

I THINK I CAN DISARM IT, SIR. I JUST--
DEET

OH, &*#^...

SSSKKKSSSHH
TAPPER!

...NO...
NOT
THIS...

OH--OH MY GOD... STEVE...

...THIS... THIS IS WHY THEY WANTED YOU HERE...?

CONTINUED IN CAPTAIN AMERICA: WINTER SOLDIER ULTIMATE COLLECTION.

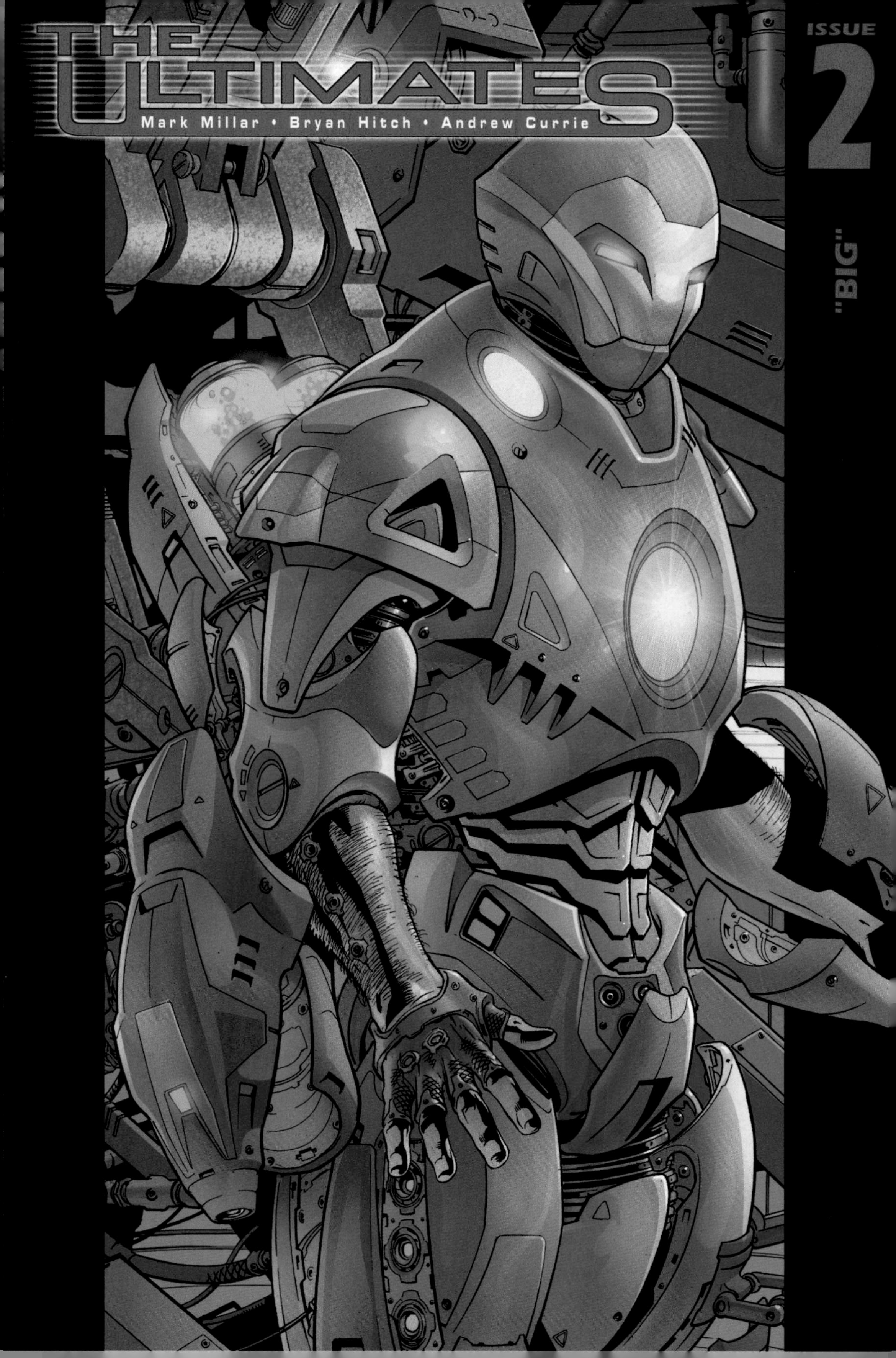

THE ULTIMATES
Mark Millar • Bryan Hitch • Andrew Currie
ISSUE
2
"BIG"

PREVIOUSLY IN THE ULTIMATES:

1945, the North Atlantic. Word had reached the Allied Forces of a terrible and destructive doomsday weapon being readied for launch against Washington, D.C.. With their forces facing defeat across Europe, this was a final act of terrorism from the remaining Nazi command designed to tear the heart out of America. In a pre-emptive strike, the Allies sent the only person capable of stopping such an attack, the hero of Omaha Beach and the Battle of Normandy. They sent Captain America. Backed by the 101st Airborne division and accompanied by War Photographer Bucky Barnes, Cap led a devastating and successful assault against the seemingly impregnable fortress that was to be the launching ground for the Nazi missile; but before they could wonder how the German forces acquired such technology, the weapon was launched.

Without a pause, Cap leaped onto the missile and was carried off as it arced into the night sky. Dropping a grenade into the propulsion jets, Cap succeeded in knocking the prototype hydrogen bomb off course, falling thousands of feet into the Arctic waters as it exploded in the upper atmosphere.

It was his final mission.

Stan Lee presents:

THE ULTIMATES

Mark Millar story

pencils Bryan Hitch   Andrew Currie inks

letters Chris Eliopoulos   Paul Mounts colors

editor Ralph Macchio   Brian Smith associate editor

editor in chief Joe Quesada   Bill Jemas president & inspiration

special thanks to Joe Kubert, Grant Morrison, and Vini Baltuttis

New York City, Today:
Are you ready to order, gentlemen?

Ah, could I have the sesame and ginger oven roast in the sweet red pepper sauce? No onions, please. They kind of bring me out in a rash.
And for you, sir?
Just the steak, thanks. Medium rare.
Thank you, sir.
MENU
Listen, I'm sorry about the view, Doctor Banner. All those little geniuses who organize my schedule and no one even stops to think about where they're sitting us for lunch.
I just hope watching them rebuild Chelsea Piers doesn't bring the whole Hulk thing back for you.
The Hulk?

Believe it or not, I hardly give the Hulk a second thought these days, General Fury.
Well, don't take this the wrong way, but I'm not entirely sure you're ready to come back yet, son. You need another six months sick leave just say the word, cowboy.
Oh, no. Believe me, sir. I really am a hundred percent again.
They've got me on three blood tests a day at the moment and there hasn't been a trace of any Hulk cells in my system for almost twelve entire weeks.
If I still seem slightly spaced, it's just that I've been popping pills to stay awake a lot lately.
Bruce Banner being asleep just feels a little too much like the Hulk being awake sometimes, if you know what I mean.

What about you? How are you enjoying the new job? Doesn't being in charge of world security get a little daunting when you're sitting in the big chair?
Man, heading S.H.I.E.L.D. is like being the Pope, the Queen and the President of the United States all rolled into one, Doctor Banner.
Even lunch with another employee becomes a minor military operation once your name's at the top of the official notepaper.
Can you believe that half these diners are highly-decorated undercover agents and whatever we select from the menu gets tested by the company bacteriologists?
Every article of clothing I had has been destroyed and replaced by a million dollar wardrobe laced with bugs and cameras.
Every word we're saying now is being taped, typed and analyzed by two hundred linguistics professors beneath a Starbucks in downtown oregon.
Taking this position was like volunteering for a career as a paranoid schizophrenic--
--but the money's good and the girls are pretty and being in charge allows me to smile favorably on all those little under-funded side-projects.
RALF & SMITTY BLEND

What are you talking about? The first Captain America won the war, saved the world and uncovered the secret alien-tech which jump-started NASA, right?

Yeah, but he also died with the riddle of the Super-Soldier serum in his veins and the closest we've come to recreating that formula was the jolly green giant back there.

Why would anyone in their right mind invest a nickel in the SSP after what I did to Chelsea Piers, General?

Because we're living in crazy times, Doctor. Crime is becoming super-crime. Terrorism is becoming super-terrorism.

Even the fattest, most stupid politician on Capitol Hill realizes that Son of Star Wars is going to be useless against the kind of problems America's really facing out there.

Serious enough to be moving your people from that damp, little squat in Pittsburgh to a brand-new facility ten miles off the coast of Manhattan, Doctor Banner.
George Junior's talking five state-sponsored super-people to begin with and I figure we need someone up there with a flag on his chest more than ever right now.
This is unbelievable: downsizing conventional numbers and reinvesting in a small, Superhuman Unit for Twenty-First Century problems.
This is everything I ever scribbled in all those faxes General Ross used to ignore. I don't know what to say, sir...
Well, don't start nibbling my ear just yet, my friend, because all your recent health problems mean that twelve-digit budget comes with a very specific condition.
Which is?
We're demoting you to Number Two.

The Super-Soldier Research Facility, Pittsburgh:
Mayflower
MOVERS
FRAGILE
Am I losing my mind here or are insects helping with the removal, Jason?
I'm sorry, Mrs. Pym, but I'm afraid that's classified information. You'll have to ask your husband if you want details about the ants.
Ants?
Yeah, what do you think, Jan? Aren't they incredible? I've got two and a half million of them clearing out the lab and another fifty thousand keeping everyone in hot drinks.
They've pretty much perfected the coffee--

--except these clumsy little iridomyrmex humilis who keep falling in when they're adding the cream and sugar.
It's a new form of military communication I've been working on using pheromones instead of radio waves to issue instructions under enemy radar.
Human trials might still be a while away, but I feel pretty confident we're just a few months from moving up to spiders.
ABANDON HOPE!
Tell me about it: I don't know if it's all the electrical storms we've been having lately or just the fact that they're moving us out of this dump--
--but the ideas for super-people are coming to me faster than I can type these days, Jan. This Giant Man formula is practically writing itself.
CAP AMERICA
You know, you're definitely on a roll again, Hank. I don't think I've seen you this super-charged about work since you built that little pacemaker for the cat.
I just wish that sweaty little Banner guy wasn't coming back to spoil everything.
Oh, don't worry about him, honey. Fury's keeping Banner busy on the other side of the complex with that Captain America serum he's been trying to crack for years.

The only time you'll even see the guy is Christmas parties and presidential visits.
Oh, I'm not scared he's going to step on our toes or anything. It's just those rumors about where his funding was coming from during the departmental lean years.
Do you really think he was involved in those secret superhuman trials on civilians? You know, like what's-his-name was saying at breakfast the other day?
Who knows?
Nobody in S.H.I.E.L.D. has a spotless record, but I think Fury was being serious when he said he wanted to drag us out of the shadows.
This super hero thing is supposed to be getting the biggest public relations push in human history and the fact that Tony Stark's involved can only be a good sign, right?
Tony Stark?
Didn't you get the e-mail?
Apparently, the Mister Clean of the Fortune 500 came down from a mountain and told Nick Fury he could have Iron Man for his nice new team.

Manhattan:
MetLife
Does he *always* show off like this when he takes the new suits out for a *spin?*
Absolutely, General Fury. Sometimes I don't think Tony considers a test run *complete* until he's waved at every *office girl* in the *city.*

OH, DON'T BELIEVE A WORD OF IT, NICK. AS OUR DEAR MISTER HOGAN IS PERFECTLY AWARE, I ONLY STOP TO WAVE AT THE VERY, VERY PRETTY ONES.
Oh, here we go again.
CAUTION
Overcompensating a little, aren't we, Master Tony?
You know what they say about bachelor boys who feel a constant compulsion to remind us what insatiable ladies men they are?
RACING
Oh, shut up and stop giving me the creeps, Jarvis. You're supposed to be the perfect English butler, for God's sake. What happened to those Vodkas and Orange I asked for?
Vodka and Orange? It's 10am, Tony.
Cheers, by the way.
Not in Moscow, old boy.

Okay, let's review this line-up S.H.I.E.L.D. is talking about:
There's me, Pym, that poor, little wife he shrunk and whatever Marine we end up with once Banner cracks the Captain America formula, correct?
That's about the size of it, Tony.
Couldn't we just lose Banner? I find it hard to put my trust in someone who turned into a green goliath and trashed Bridget Fonda's favorite New York patisserie.
Out of the question, Daddio. The team needs a leader and Bruce Banner is still our best chance of turning a top U.S. soldier into the new Captain America, my friend.
What about this Thor guy over in Europe? Did you see that anti-corporate piece he did for 60 Minutes a couple of nights ago? He's wonderfully charismatic.
But still not answering his mobile, unfortunately. That said, with a hammer like that, I'd rather have him with us than against us, if you know what I mean.
Have you talked to the Fantastic Four?
After all the negative press they've been getting from their neighbors lately? Don't even think about it, cowboy.
The budget cuts we're making in the regular army are going to make us a political hot potato as it is. Why do you think I'm not risking any mutants in the initial line-up?

Is that why you were so keen to get me onboard? Do I bring a little rented respectability to the party, General?
Never made a secret of it, Tony. You're a trusted brand name in everything from internet software to aspartame-polluted diet soda.
And, of course, this new Iron Man armor you devised in the mountains doesn't exactly hurt your case either.
Light-negativity, thought-scramblers, a tracking-system that could find a Democrat in Texas-- this is everything we S.H.I.E.L.D. boys ever fantasized about, man.
You mean besides the record-breaking contracts Stark International just secured?
The only thing we're losing sleep over right now is why you changed your mind about sharing the Iron Man tech with my big, bad military-industrial complex.
Don't try telling me it was the contracts, Tony. Everyone and his mother knows you've got twice as much money as God. Why the one hundred and eighty degrees?
In all seriousness?
STOP

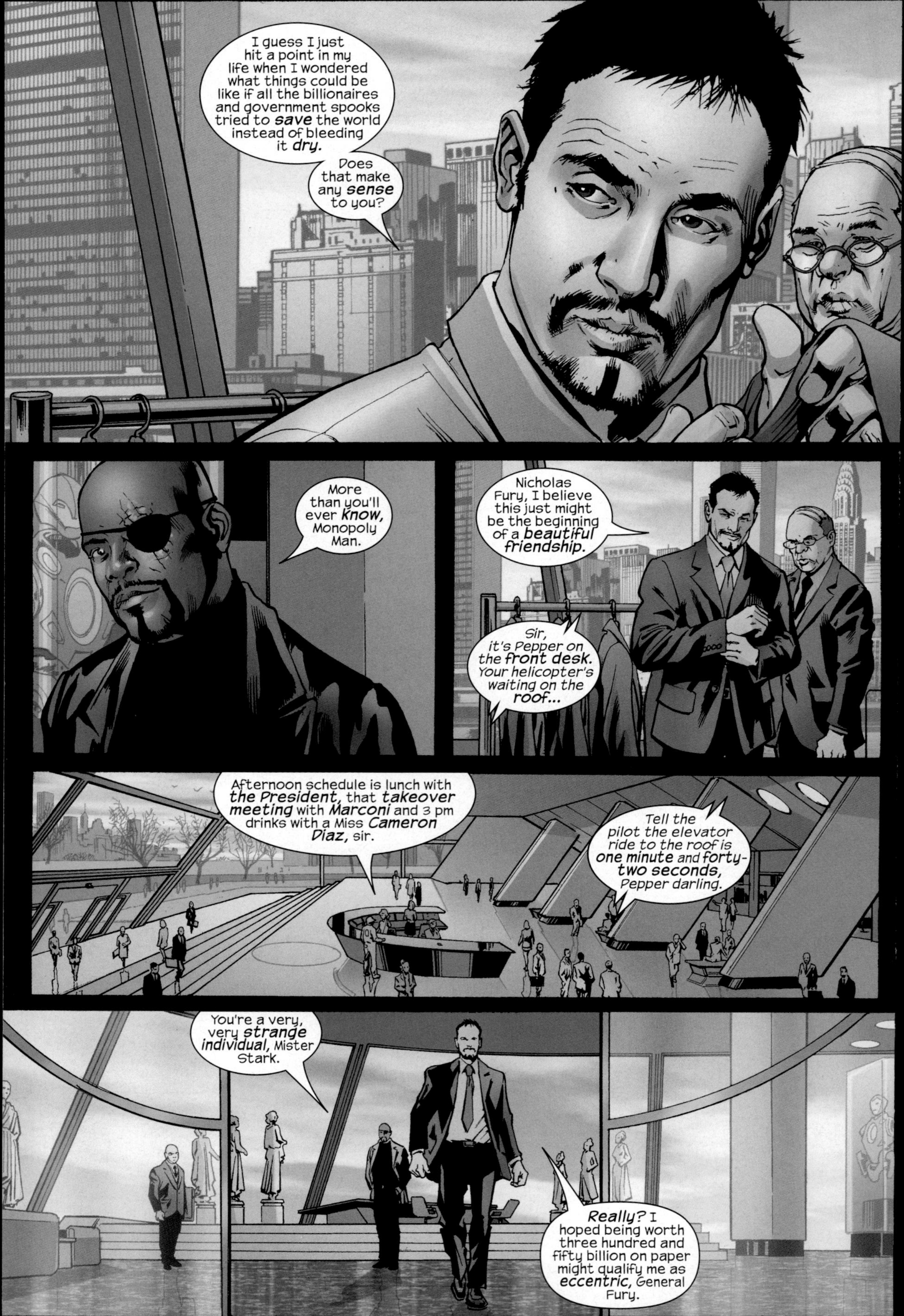
I guess I just hit a point in my life when I wondered what things could be like if all the billionaires and government spooks tried to *save* the world instead of bleeding it *dry*.
Does that make any *sense* to you?
More than you'll ever *know*, Monopoly Man.
Nicholas Fury, I believe this just might be the beginning of a *beautiful friendship*.
Sir, it's Pepper on the *front desk*. Your helicopter's waiting on the *roof*...
Afternoon schedule is lunch with *the President*, that *takeover meeting* with *Marconi* and 3 pm drinks with a Miss *Cameron Diaz*, sir.
Tell the pilot the elevator ride to the roof is **one minute** and **forty-two seconds**, Pepper darling.
You're a very, very *strange individual*, Mister Stark.
Really? I hoped being worth three hundred and fifty billion on paper might qualify me as *eccentric*, General Fury.

The Triskelion, Upper Bay Manhattan:
Nice to meet you again, Doctor Banner. Would you like a hand with that luggage? It looks kind of heavy.
No, thank you, Mrs Pym. I might not be The Hulk anymore, but I think I'm more than capable of carrying a few books and a laptop.
Suit yourself.
So what do you think of the new facility? I know it's only half-finished, but even this is a million times better than that rat-hole in Pittsburgh.
How you managed to work all those years in that place without going nuts I'll never know.
You mean turning green and going on a rampage through New York doesn't qualify as nuts anymore?

That was a joke, by the way, Mrs. Pym.
Uh, yeah. Good one.
Oh, listen. I almost forgot: I couldn't believe it when Nick Fury told me you were engaged to Betty Ross.
Did you know she and I used to room together back at NYU before she switched to Berkeley for that communications degree?
God, I haven't seen Betty since they released all those special editions of the Star Wars movies. I can't believe Fury's hired her as our Director of Communications.
To be honest, we haven't been a couple for quite some time, Mrs. Pym. Betty bought one of those stupid self-analysis books a few months ago and decided I was a toxic influence.
The last time I saw her, she'd moved to SOHO, dyed her hair pink and suggested she and I try a temporary relationship break for six months.
Really?
I can't imagine why.

Hey, Bruce. Sorry I couldn't meet you from the helicopter, but these workaholics have been prepping me for the Giant-Man trials all morning.
Yeah, right. Like we get to make any of the decisions around here. Good to see you back on your feet again, Doctor Banner.
Let's hope you're luckier than I was with Captain America, Dr. Pym. I suppose your biggest concern with something like this is that everything grows at the same speed, huh?
Oh no. I've got the biology worked out to the tenth decimal point. I'm just worried if I'll be able to stop growing before I hit that critical sixty feet mark.
Why? What's the significance of that?
Sixty feet is the exact height at which the human skeleton can no longer support its own body-mass, Doctor.
That big baby of mine is worried his thigh-bones are going to snap even though I've told him a million times that stopping will be an automatic reflex.
What do you think keeps me from shrinking smaller than an inch, honey? Our neurology won't let us change size to the point where the physical body is in danger.
Well, it's time to put that pillow-talk of ours to the test, sweetheart.

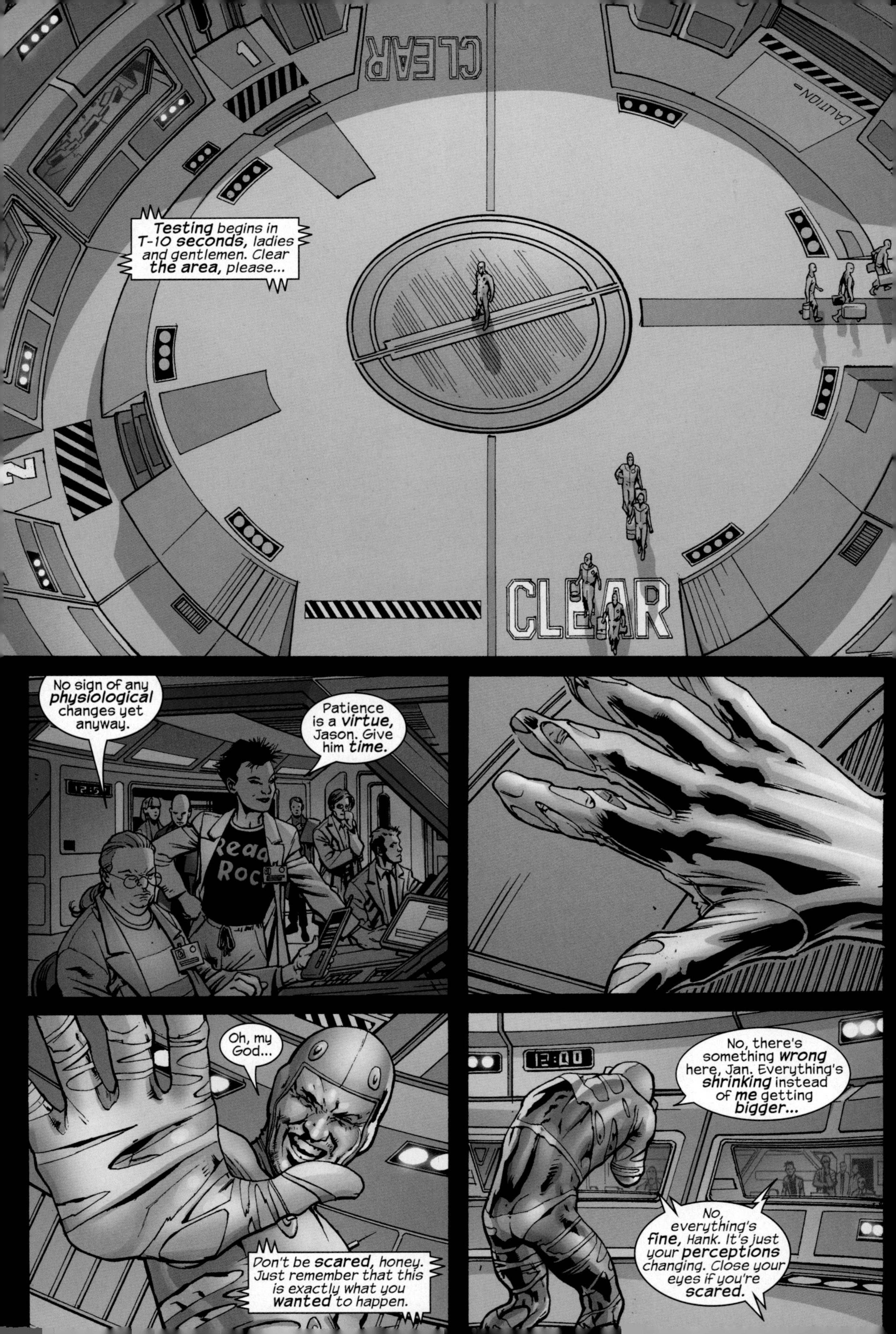

CLEAR
CAUTION
Testing begins in T-10 seconds, ladies and gentlemen. Clear the area, please...
CLEAR
No sign of any physiological changes yet anyway.
Patience is a virtue, Jason. Give him time.
Oh, my God...
Don't be scared, honey. Just remember that this is exactly what you wanted to happen.
No, there's something wrong here, Jan. Everything's shrinking instead of me getting bigger...
No, everything's fine, Hank. It's just your perceptions changing. Close your eyes if you're scared.

JAN! WHAT HAPPENED TO THE LIGHTS?
Nothing to worry about, honey. Just a little technical glitch. Support: shut down the power along tracks forty-seven and forty-eight and hit the floor-lights, please.
OH MY GOD! OH MY GOD! I'M TURNING INSIDE-OUT, JAN! STOP THE EXPERIMENT! I'M TURNING INSIDE-OUT!
What are you waiting for, you numbskull?
Hit the blasted lights!

Gotcha, suckers.
CAUTION

Hank Pym, I'm gonna kick your--
Fifty-nine feet, eleven and a half inches?
Way to go, Dr. Pym!
Oh, man! On a scale of one to ten, how much did that rock, Doctor Banner?
Oh, ten, Jason. Definitely ten.
Yee-hah.

Dr. Banner's Quarters:
How am I doing? How do you think I'm doing, General?
Hank Pym is swaggering around and calling himself Giant-Man and I'm sitting here with a bottle of wine and scribbling useless equations all over a foolscap pad.
Why am I letting this guy just walk all over me like this? He's going to end up creating the whole blasted team if I don't crack this idiotic Super-Soldier formula soon.
And why can't I open my mouth to these people without coming off like a complete and utter...
Buffy
Excuse me, General?
I said shut up and crack open that bottle of Champagne you've been saving for the next season of Star Trek, Doctor Banner. The answer to your prayers has just been answered...

"...You're not going to believe what they've just fished out of the Arctic Ocean."
CONTINUED IN THE ULTIMATES ULTIMATE COLLECTION.

CAPTAIN AMERICA

CAPTAIN AMERICA #6 VARIANT
BY STEVE EPTING & FRANK D'ARMATA

The English Channel
SO, YOU WANT US TO STAY HERE, THEN, SIR?
YES. WHAT I HAVE TO DO HERE, I NEED TO DO ON MY OWN.

IF YOU DON'T MIND ME ASKING, SIR...
THIS ISLAND'S NOT ON ANY OF THE CHARTS, AND WE NEEDED S.H.I.E.L.D. CLEARANCE JUST TO LAND...BUT OTHER THAN THAT OLD CASTLE UP THERE, IT LOOKS DESERTED.
WHAT IS THIS PLACE?

THIS IS WHERE I DIED.

SO MANY CONFLICTING REPORTS ABOUT THAT DAY...THE DAY EVERYTHING WENT WRONG...SO MANY FALSE DETAILS LEAKED FOR TOP SECRET REASONS. I'VE READ THEM ALL.
SOME SAY IT ALL TOOK PLACE IN ENGLAND. ONE REPORT I READ CLAIMED WE WERE BROUGHT TO NEWFOUNDLAND.
SOMETIMES I THINK I'M NOT EVEN SURE WHAT REALLY HAPPENED ANYMORE.

DID I EVER REALLY REMEMBER ANY OF IT, OR WAS I JUST FILLING IN BLANKS?
LIKE AN ACCIDENT VICTIM WHO DOESN'T REMEMBER ANYTHING AFTER GETTING IN THEIR CAR UNTIL THEY WAKE UP IN THE HOSPITAL...

NO...I ALWAYS REMEMBERED ZEMO AND THE DRONE PLANE...
ALWAYS REMEMBERED IT EXPLODING.

BUT THE REST OF IT, I SUPPOSE IT'S POSSIBLE THAT READING REPORTS ABOUT THAT DAY COLORED MY PERCEPTIONS.

ALL I KNOW FOR SURE IS, THESE NEW MEMORIES THAT HAVE BEEN SURFACING-- MEMORIES OF ZEMO CAPTURING US, TORTURING BUCKY...
THEY FEEL FAR TOO REAL...

LIKE SOMETHING'S UNLOCKING THE PART OF MY BRAIN WHERE THEY'VE HIDDEN ALL THIS TIME AND FORCING ME TO ACKNOWLEDGE THEM.
THAT'S WHY I HAD TO COME HERE, AFTER ALL THESE YEARS...TO FIND THE TRUTH.

THIS ISLAND IS ONLY IN ONE REPORT ABOUT THAT DAY. THE ONE PREPARED FOR PRESIDENT ROOSEVELT.

THIS WAS A NAZI BASE BETWEEN OCCUPIED FRANCE AND ALLIED BRITAIN. EVEN AFTER THE NAZIS WERE DRIVEN OUT OF FRANCE, THEY MANAGED TO KEEP THIS SPOT A SECRET.
AND WHEN ZEMO CAPTURED US IN ENGLAND, HE AND HIS MEN BROUGHT US HERE, HELD US CAPTIVE WHILE THEY ANALYZED THE ALLIED DRONE PLANE THEY'D STOLEN.

BUT UNTIL THESE PAST FEW WEEKS, I NEVER REMEMBERED THE BRUTALITY OF THE TIME WE WERE HERE. YET...
NO. MY GOD...

THIS IS THE ROOM. THIS IS WHERE IT HAPPENED... I WAS FORCED TO WATCH--
GET THE HELL AWAY FROM HIM!
HA HA HA HA HA HA!

--AND ZEMO...HE WOULDN'T STOP LAUGHING.
HA HA HA HA HA HA!

HOW COULD I HAVE FORGOTTEN SOMETHING LIKE THIS...?

MAYBE A BETTER QUESTION IS...WHY AM I REMEMBERING IT ALL NOW?

--AMERIKANER!

--AMERIKANER!
BUDDABUDDABUDD

WHAT--? NAZI SOLDIERS?

ZEMO? NO, WHAT IS--THIS ISN'T REAL... IT CAN'T BE.
KAPITAN AMERIKANER!
GET HIM! KILL HIM!